YO-BEB-032

Culture Gulch

By John Canaday

CULTURE GULCH
EMBATTLED CRITIC
KEYS TO ART
    (with Katherine H. Canaday)
MAINSTREAMS OF MODERN ART
THE METROPOLITAN SEMINARS IN ART

John
Canaday

Culture
Gulch

Notes on Art and Its
Public in the 1960's

Farrar, Straus and Giroux
NEW YORK

Contents

DEDICATION: *To Brooks Atkinson*   3

FOREWORD: *Author to Reader*   7

1 *The State of Art and Some Artists*

The Camera Did It. Why Deny It?   17
Kenneth Noland: Straw Without Bricks   19
Not Quite Able to Feel Sorry for Grace Hartigan   25
Young Italians, Indeed!   29
This Way to the Big Erotic Art Show   33
Jan Lebenstein and the Mysterious Visitors   36
Julius Bissier   41
Juan Genovés: Violence and Anonymity   45
Edward Hopper: Antaeus, and the Loneliness of a
    Long-Distance Runner   50
Venice on the Potomac   56
"F-111" and the Day the House Caught Fire   63

2 *Letting Off Steam*

How Come   77
Nix on Barnett Newman's Stations of the Cross   79
Out of Patience with Robert Motherwell   82
I Got Those Yves Klein Blues   84
Our National Pride: The World's Worst Sculpture   88
Goodby, Mrs. Gumboil   96

3 *The More or Less Recent Past, or Far Away and Long Ago in the Twentieth Century*

Pascin and a Fact of Life   103
The Germanness of Max Beckmann   107
Fernand Léger Is Alive and Well   114
Gaston Lachaise: A Major Reservation, Hesitantly Offered   120
Marsden Hartley as a Gap-Closer   124

4 *Four Personalities*

Grandma Moses   133
James Rorimer   136
Fiske Kimball   139
A Bouquet for Miss Belmont   144

5 *Money Troubles*

The Auction Game, or, The Lost Innocence of Mr. Baddleigh Taken   151
The Vanity Racket, or, The Sad Dream World of Gordon Gullible   158
Car-Wash Culture, or, Big Problems Come in Small Museums   163

6 *Reportage*

Picasso in the Wilderness   185
Gopher Prairie Irredenta   192
Ginevra de' Benci, the Ill-Natured Debutante   195
Florence After the Flood   199

Epilogue   209

List of Illustrations

EDWARD KIENHOLZ: *Five Dollar Billy* 11
KENNETH NOLAND: *One Way* 21
GRACE HARTIGAN: *Jolie* 27
MICHELANGELO PISTOLETTO: *Man Looking at Negative* 30
JAN LEBENSTEIN: *Axial Figure 111* 37
JULIUS BISSIER: *14. August 60K* 42
JUAN GENOVÉS: *Man Alone* 46
JUAN GENOVÉS: *Angulo 18°* 48
EDWARD HOPPER: *Hotel Room* 51
EDWARD HOPPER: *New York Movie* 53
FRANK GALLO: *Girl on Couch* 59
RED GROOMS: *Chicago* 62
JAMES ROSENQUIST: *F-111* 64
JAMES ROSENQUIST: *F-111* (detail) 67
BARNETT NEWMAN: *The Voice* 81
ROBERT MOTHERWELL: *Elegy to the Spanish Republic, No. 78* 82
YVES KLEIN, *fire-painting* 86
DONALD DE LUE: *Spirit of American Youth* 89
BRUCE MOORE: *Female Figure* 92
WHEELER WILLIAMS: *Airman* 93
ALBINO MANCA: *Eagle* 94
JULES PASCIN: *Anne Harvey* 105
MAX BECKMANN: *Self-Portrait, Florence* 109
MAX BECKMANN: *Self-Portrait with Horn* 110

MAX BECKMANN: *Self-Portrait in Blue Jacket*   112
FERNAND LÉGER: *Composition au vase de fleurs*   115
FERNAND LÉGER: *La Jeune Indienne*   117
GASTON LACHAISE, photographed with *Elevation*   123
MARSDEN HARTLEY: *Fox Island, Maine*   126
GRANDMA MOSES, 1959   134
JAMES RORIMER, 1963   137
FISKE KIMBALL, 1949   141
PABLO PICASSO: sculpture in Civic Center, Chicago   187
LEONARDO DA VINCI: *Ginevra de' Benci*   196

Culture Gulch

There have been many satisfactions in working for *The New York Times* during the past ten years, but nothing has given me more delight, mixed in this case with a moment of disbelief, than a note that came in the house mail one morning welcoming me to the paper, expressing approval of my first columns, and signed "Brooks Atkinson." That was in 1959. Late in 1964, inspired by no occasion that I can remember, I wrote the following piece about Brooks on the backs of a couple of envelopes while waiting for an order of scrambled eggs at an institution called Gough's Chop House across the street from the *Times*'s West 43rd Street entrance, and offered it to Ruth Adler, editor of our house organ, which is called *Times Talk*. She published it under the title "Babbling about Brooks," and *Variety* reprinted it (another thrill). I offer it here by way of dedicating this collection of *Times* pieces to an admired friend, trusting that no one will ask, as one befuddled staff member did, "What has Canaday got against Brooks Atkinson, anyway?"

It has been five years now that I've been sitting around *The New York Times* twiddling my thumbs and watching how the place operates, and I think somebody should tell the truth about Brooks Atkinson. After all, the guy isn't God and it's high time somebody said so.

In the first place, where would he ever have got without

that name of his? It's that "Brooks" that does the trick, with its double connotation of conservative high-class haberdashery and babbling waters in a sylvan countryside. Never has so great a reputation hung so firmly on a happy combination of six letters, or only five if you count the "o" just once.

By regular attendance night after night for about a million years, Brooks Atkinson created the impression that he knew something about the theater to such an extent that any marquee bearing the legend "Not bad—Atkinson—Times" was set for a six-year run. And by checking his sentences against an elementary grammar book B. A. created the illusion that he knew something about the use of the English language, to such an extent that kids like me used to try to emulate him before they wised up. Trouble was, he never bothered to explain to us where sentences come from, which is simply from the intimate conjunction of a subject and a predicate.

All this while his only firsthand connection with the theater has been a boyhood experience as sound-effects man in a primitive nickelodeon up in some New England hamlet where he used to rub two pieces of sandpaper together to make like an approaching train. He told me so himself. Of course, it was a job that took a certain degree of coordination, but is that genius?

No.

The ironic thing is, and it shows just how much you can get away with on this newspaper if you know how to put up the right front, that everybody has always been fully aware of what B. A. is really interested in. When he should have been boning up on Plautus and Shakespeare he was out talking to birds, whistling and warbling and cheeping and carrying on in the worst kind of way when all he would have had to do would be give a nod and he could have had every chick on Broadway in his hair.

Incidentally, he has depended a lot on a full head of hair to create the personality on which he continues to draw his salary, and naturally some of the rest of us resent it. He sits there at his desk under that mop, with that pipe and that tweed jacket as auxiliary props, and he looks so much like the real thing that he's managed to fool everybody around the place, even including Clara Rotter.*

Honestly, the *Times* might as well shut down if it can't do better than this. Since it can't, it might as well keep publishing, in a hopeless kind of way. But why not face things and change the name to *The Times-Atkinson*?

---

* This "in" reference must be explained for outsiders. Miss Rotter, a tough-minded Amazonian type, carries the entire weight of the *Times* Drama Desk on her shoulders and has never had the wool pulled over her eyes except by B.A.

Culture Gulch extends from one end to the other of the U.S.A., but the name was coined at *The New York Times* to designate an area on the third floor where critics, reporters, and other staff members assigned to covering the arts are segregated. "Culture Gulch" is an appropriate title for this book not only because all the pieces collected in it were written in my line of duty as *Times* art critic, but also because most of them are concerned with art in the 1960's—its practitioners, its promoters, and its public—which exists in a kind of gulch, a cultural ravine, a low spot between the high bank of the past and, by optimistic presumption, the high bank of the future. In addition, the connotation with rootin' tootin' don't-take-'em-serious Westerns is appropriate to the air of fraudulent excitement generated these days by dealers, museums, and, alas, critics, to stimulate an audience for their product. Hence the irreverent *Culture Gulch* (*faute-de-pire,* as one third-floor colleague likes to put it) in spite of my conviction that the art of painting, no matter what vicissitudes it must pass through from time to time, is the surest evidence that man's strengths outweigh his follies in the long run.

Culture Gulch follows a similar volume of pieces from the *Times* and elsewhere called *Embattled Critic,* published in 1962. At that time, as a newcomer, I was not really embattled, which means arrayed for battle, but I was sorely beleaguered. Certain other critics, joined by a number of collectors who had invested heavily in a kind of painting that I thought overrated, and any number of artists engaged in fabricating the merchandise, loathed me because in my innocence I had been unable to regard abstract expressionism as the culminating glory of Western art, and had said so. I had also suggested that dealers who promoted new art forms were not necessarily to be identified with Father Damien, giving up all to join the lepers. These ideas did not sit well in New York, to my genuine astonishment.

Whether or not the subsequent disintegration of the abstract expressionist cartel of painters, dealers, and critics was hastened by some of the *Times* articles reprinted in *Embattled Critic* I do not know, but I am sure that the school's virtual demise certainly was not the direct result of anything I wrote. Abstract expressionism was an overripe fruit ready to fall off the branch and I happened to touch it just then. And in truth I never questioned abstract expressionism's legitimacy as an honest idea. I questioned only the nature of the proselytization that inflated one minor aesthetic to such outrageous proportions that more important standards were rejected or thrown out of kilter.

But all of that is past. Things move quickly and are forgotten quickly in New York, and much of *Embattled Critic* deals with arguments that have been either settled or abandoned. I have tried to make up this new book from material that will not age too rapidly, but it seems appropriate to begin it with some comments on the scene at the moment of gathering the pieces together. The following article appeared in the *Times* of September 22, 1968, under the title "Looking Forward to Not Getting All Wrought Up This Season, Thank You" and shows how things have changed during the few years, 1962 to 1969, between publication of *Embattled Critic* and this book:

People are complaining that it looks like a dull season coming up in the galleries. The excitement has gone out of the art scene, they say. If by "excitement" they mean what I mean, I am inclined to agree that it has diminished—and a good thing, too.

The sources that manufacture excitement—the most aggressive dealers engaged in synthesizing new reputations and the most fashion-minded curators who follow their lead—seem to be taking breathers, the former perhaps from exhaustion of material, and the latter in recognition of an exhaustion of public interest. You can go on for just so long assuring the public that your current selection of what we used to call avant-garde art is the most exciting thing that ever happened. For just so long you can keep the public convinced that each year's sensation is the biggest thing since Giotto. Eventually even the most gullible audience begins to ask what ever happened to what's-his-name, who was last year's big innovator.

We seem to have reached some such saturation point, and if we are in for a season of drying out, nothing could be healthier. For a couple of years, the encouraging thing about the art scene has been its increasing variety. The most highly publicized schools of recent years—abstract expressionism, pop, and op——have been brought into some kind of balance as their hangers-on have been eliminated by a form of aesthetic Darwinism. Calmer appraisals by critics who once bubbled, and by curators of propagandizing museums who must balance gate receipts against aesthetic values, have followed the line of the unquestionable umpire in such games

—the buying collector, who is beginning to learn a new caution in a crazy market.

It is encouraging, too, that during the 1960's there have been strong independent artists (Richard Lindner is a single example) who have come into full recognition in spite of the competition of the circus troupes—sometimes, as in Mr. Lindner's case, after too many years, but sometimes too as debutants. Half a dozen minor movements or continuations of major movements once considered passé (constructivist continuations in sculpture, surrealist-derived fantasies, and even some respectable figurative art outside the realm of fantasy) have shown how firmly rooted these recent traditions are. They have held their own while the wild top growth of overfed excitement has wilted and dropped away.

One artist commented recently that it takes a lot of bad art to produce a little that is good. This is often true. The cellars of Italian museums are filled with puerile Renaissance paintings, and thousands of others have disappeared through the action of a benevolent natural law that tends to conserve the best work of an age and do away with its fluff. Seeing too much fluff in the galleries during a typical season, we despair of the state of art today and recognize the rivalries of different schools as a war of pygmies. But there are artists like Edward Kienholz who, because they are classifiable only in a combination of wildly split categories (Mr. Kienholz is part surrealist, part pop artist, part social polemicist and altogether a poet of horror), rise above any category and justify whatever puerilities have been part of the foundations on which such an artist works.

That Mr. Kienholz's conspicuousness has developed coincidentally with that of his antipode, Kenneth Noland, is sufficient indication that no school just now has anything comparable to the stranglehold that abstract expressionism enjoyed ten years ago. The cool school to which Mr. Noland belongs is currently triumphant as the new thing, but in its cool way it offers itself to the public on a take-it-or-leave-it basis, rather than the take-it-or-else approach adopted by other recent schools in their missionary fervor.

This comes as a relief to a public that has been fatigued by a series of conversions from one excitement to the next, and may have accounted in part for the drop in gallery attendance last season. The combination of relief and dis-

EDWARD KIENHOLZ: *Five Dollar Billy,* 1960-61.
Photograph courtesy of the Dwan Gallery, New York.

enchantment was further supported just at the season's end by the comedy of the Venice Biennale. That fiasco confirmed an idea that the public once held but had been educated to discard—the idea that contemporary art is a lot of flimflam. Suddenly the paramount exhibition of contemporary art was denounced as aesthetically corrupt, politically fascist, and basely commercial—denounced not by members of a frustrated old guard who had been calling it evil names for years, but by Italian students as young rebels. What could be more discouraging to the assiduous art lover than to spend years learning to respond to contemporary art, only to learn that all he has learned to appreciate has become old hat?

An art critic for an out-of-town newspaper made an appalling comment (not repeated in print so far as I know) after trudging through the Whitney's summer show of paintings by artists under forty. The show was in effect a review of the heavings and strainings that have characterized American art of the 1960's in its effort to prove itself to itself with one excitement after another. "Oh, why don't they just go on and let it *die?*" this critic asked, reneging for the moment the assumption that a critic's job is to assure the public that art is worth troubling with just because it is art, and that it is even more worth the trouble if it is new, or tries to be.

The assumption has become a vicious one because it has been applied unselectively with too much enthusiasm. Yet it is a necessary assumption: blind faith in the function of art, even when it is in a mess like the current one, is necessary if the whole thing is not to be chucked. You can go through what seems to have been the messiest of seasons but at the end of it you recognize how good some of the spots were. You also realize how distorted your point of view can become when, out of sheer weariness with making objections, you tolerate as acceptable art more than about one per cent of the work being shown by living artists. (History has already weeded out ninety-nine per cent of the art of the past, which is one reason it looks so good.) To say that the prospect of an unexciting season is a happy prospect is not to be perverse, but rather to give a vote of confidence that art can sustain itself even when deprived of the artificial stimulants upon which we have taught it to depend.

Let me add that the pieces included here have not been doctored to take advantage of second-guessing. They are as they appeared except for the deletion of a few incidental factual references (such as the addresses of galleries or museums) usually given in a newspaper report but not pertinent in a book, and as changed by bits of surgery when two articles were fused into one (which explains why some articles carry two dates). Here and there I have furtively substituted a better word or phrase for one that was the best I could think of at the time of writing, and I have also introduced a sentence or two now and then to make up for some that were deleted in publication when an article ran beyond its allotted space. But I have not cheated.

1

*The State of Art
and Some Artists*

The Camera Did It. Why Deny It?

With an insistence that is surely self-defensive, abstract painters and their most enthusiastic supporters among critics refuse to admit that the invention of photography dictated a direction that painting had to take by default. "Art would have gone abstract anyway," they insist. "It was obviously inevitable."

I cannot see it that way—although, playing the pointless game of "what do you suppose would have happened if," I can see that painting in our century might have developed an abstract subdivision in the inconceivable circumstance of the camera's never having been born. But the camera's invasion of a world that had been the painter's domain since prehistoric times created changes so fundamental, preempting the foundation upon which painting had always rested, that we must recognize the calamitous truth that painting in the twentieth century has been mostly a matter of redesigning a weakened superstructure.

Is it not possible that the camera's reproductive eye robbed painting of its primary reason for being and forced it little by little into the isolated position it now holds in our lives? Everyone knows that no painting worth very much has limited itself to simple reproduction of the look of the world, yet some of the early Flemings with their heightened realism and some of the impressionists with their light-shattered landscapes (two examples among hundreds) depended as much on the look of things as on their interpretation to create an art of expressive significance.

In different ways, painters until our century were practitioners of a variety of magic that belonged to painting alone, the magic that transferred onto a small flat surface an immense world that exists in space and depth. When only men could do this, their painted worlds held a kind of magic that must have affected people's way of seeing even the least imaginative painting. But when a machine learned to do it, the magic was gone. The effect of the camera was not merely to outdate the artist as a recording technician—this was not important—but to reduce his stature as a magician.

At this point you can argue in either of two directions. You can say that photography was a purification that painting had awaited for centuries, painting's final release from its bondage to visual imagery. But if this had been bondage, how odd that painters never fretted under it. They seem rather to have gloried in response to the look of the world while they also gloried in the elements of painting by which they modified it—adjustments of color and form—appropriately to their responses.

When we say that the visual world became exhausted as expressive raw material about fifty years ago, we are only making a convenient assumption. The truth might be that with the perfection of the camera in the service of mass printing, the glut of photographs under our eyes everywhere, everywhere, every minute year after year—do you realize how many you see in a single day—has so deeply brutalized our way of seeing the world that painters, being only people, have lost their capacity to respond to the world as a visual phenomenon.

Photographs used to be a reflection of the world, but now

we see the world in terms of photographs. Cartier-Bresson or any great photographer may reveal the world, but a million other photographers, including every child with a camera, obscure it. For a painter, the change is not so much that he need not paint the world for us because the camera can picture it more readily, but that he cannot paint it for himself because the camera has vitiated his way of seeing.

In this case photography has not liberated the painter into the realm of pure art, but has robbed him. He is left with pure form and pure color, and he is left free to manipulate them in abstract exercises for the special pleasure the manipulation may give him. There can be a kind of magic here, too, but it is an odd, inconclusive kind. The gestures, the manipulations of paraphernalia, seem always on the verge of producing a revelation, but in the end nothing happens and the performance must be accepted as an end in itself.

June 10, 1962

Kenneth Noland: Straw Without Bricks

Kenneth Noland is an artist, eminently successful at the moment, who, however great his success and however impressive his achievement within its acknowledged limitations, exemplifies the tragic position of the abstract painter, a position that is often called a glorious liberation. Mr. Noland's paintings consist of chevrons (formerly concentric circles)* of pure color. Thus his is primarily an art of "color

---

* As of 1968, Mr. Noland's chevrons have been replaced by horizontal stripes.

decision." Any color in any Noland could be changed to another color and although this would produce, as he says, "a different painting," pure trial and error would produce some acceptable Nolands in the hands of anyone ignorant of color theory or even of a feeling for color. Mr. Noland himself destroys as many paintings as he exhibits.

The trouble with an art of color decision is that color decision has always been a concern of the artist along with line decision, form decision, relationships decision, space decision, iconographical decision, and a dozen other decisions taken for granted as preliminaries in the creation of paintings summarizing some philosophical statement of consequence pegged to a dictated subject. That the contemporary artist can be content, or reconciled, to fencing himself off into so small an area of what was once a limitless field, is incomprehensible to me.

Abstract art, for all the pleasure it can afford the specialist, is an admission that (in the words of one abstract painter) "there is so much exhaustion around that I am compelled to recognize it." Mr. Noland recognizes this exhaustion but is obviously happy in accepting it as a point of departure inward. What I cannot understand is why any man feels compelled, under these circumstances, to become a painter and dig deeper into a dry well, when industrial design, architecture, and the movies—all of them living arts where his talent could be used—are open to him.

The common argument in favor of abstract art is that it reduces art to its essentials. This is true in a way. If you are interested in art as an experience in pure theory, the essentials of theory are there, stripped naked. For anyone who wants to fight about it, let it be known that this writer, a specialist of sorts, owns and consistently enjoys several

KENNETH NOLAND: *One Way,* 1964. 100″ high. Acrylic on canvas. Collection of Mr. and Mrs. Philip M. Stern, Washington, D.C. Photograph courtesy of André Emmerich Gallery, New York.

abstract paintings. But this reduction of art to pure theory is not a reduction to essentials, but to incidentals, the substitution of means for the end, and ultimately an admission that the contemporary world offers no meaningful goal for the painter's endeavors.

By this admission, the painter can only—resorting here

to what has already become a cliché—paint about painting. Art of this kind is the safest art in the world. It is subject to no definable standards of excellence, it cannot be called either right or wrong, successful or unsuccessful, except by the artist's own judgment by standards that he may apply with intelligence and integrity, but standards that, as far as the work of art is concerned, are as adaptable to the defense of one painting as of another, hence eliminating any difference between the significant and the trivial. The artist becomes the dictator of personal esoteric standards rather than the creative professional who accepts the legitimacy of universal standards and elevates them by personal application. His intention becomes identical with his production, whatever that production may turn out to be. Whatever happens must be accepted as what was supposed to have happened. Whether or not there was any good reason for it to have happened at all becomes beside the point.

This narrowness, where the artist takes a tiny fragment of what used to be total expression, is comparable to the cutting up of a holy garment, the worshipping of a thread from the shroud of a saint, with the idea that it has miraculous powers, a concept that has nothing to do with the totality of the saint and his life. There is no wholeness here but only a veneration for what was once a wholeness, and a willingness to accept any fragmentation as the best possible compromise in a clutching toward something no longer attainable.

Becoming an abstract painter is like entering the monastery of an order where the indulgence of any private mania becomes the insignia of acceptance into the brotherhood, where the degree of the extremity in the indulgence is likely to be the measure of merit as applied by an international coterie of critics and award-giving juries. Mr. Noland is a happy artist and I wish him a continuation of that happiness, but his position seems to me a pathetic one. He is the artist as an isolated man, working in a field where his success must be in inverse ratio to his contact with the profundity of those human values that keep the world turning.

The children of Israel, in bondage to Egypt, were forced to make bricks without straw, the binder that held them together. Mr. Noland and his colleagues are in a reverse position. With plenty of straw, they have no clay, the solid stuff that makes the bricks that make a building. This may be the fault of their bondage to the twentieth century—certainly there are more good abstract painters around than there are good figurative painters, a thumping proof that abstract art has been the art of our time. But that in itself is the saddest possible comment on what it means to be a painter today.

In an article in *The New York Times* of August 25, 1968, Mr. Noland was quoted in terms that boiled down to "The thing in painting is color." Mr. Noland in the same article objected to phrase-making, so we must not saddle him with this aphorism, yet it is the heart of his idea of what painting is, and very nearly the whole of it. And it sounds good at first. One thinks of Matisse as Mr. Noland's precursor, then of Renoir as Matisse's, and then back to Delacroix, and from Delacroix to Rubens.

But like so many aphorisms, including political slogans, "The thing in painting is color" settles for effective expression of a fractional truth as if it were a whole one, and hence is less than fractionally valid. Color is *not* what painting is all about even in the work of Mr. Noland's immediate predecessor, Morris Louis, and certainly not what the painting of Grandfather Jackson Pollock is all about. As for Matisse, Renoir, Delacroix, Rubens, and any other colorists you want to mention, they were fascinated or even obsessed by color, but that is not nearly what their painting is all about.

Except as our perspective is distorted by this tiny pigmented mote in our eye just now, by this starved, sterile, parasitic art so interestingly born, bred, and maintained in an incubator by the dealers and critics who sell it, painting is all about life and thought, about gods and heroes, and about buffoons and villains, and about ordinary people in between. Painting is all about the look of the world and what lies beneath it, about elysiums that painters have patched together and other painters have demolished. Painting is all about greatness, paltriness, cruelty, faith, hope, frustration, delusion, and discovery—about everything, expressed as miserable banalities in the work of little men, and as summaries of human experience in the art of great ones.

And there's the catch. For whatever reason, the miserable banalities are too much with us today in the work of painters who bring us a message. The dreadful phrase "bring us a message" in itself tells what is wrong: an emasculating self-consciousness besets most contemporary artists who set out to make comments on life. At best they stammer. More often they turn either fretful or pompous. It is obvious that, admirably, they have decided they want to say something. But alas, that too often is the only idea they have. Better one of Mr. Noland's perfectly baked fractional loaves of plastic bread than the depressing, soggy mass of dough offered us by most painters who try to deal with life.

November 15, 1964, and November 10, 1968

Not Quite Able to Feel Sorry for Grace Hartigan

Sometimes you feel sorry for artists. Sometimes, of course, they bother you like anything with their defensive arrogance and their oddly innocent attitude toward things. But after all, they are in a difficult position. The artist, once upon a time, was an imperatively needed man but is now a dangling one. Once he was able to create visual statements of a unifying philosophy (or religion) or to be a creative recorder of visual fact. But today, as a philosopher, he lives in an age that does not know what it believes, and as a recorder of fact he has, of course, been long since killed stone cold dead by the camera.

You hear talk today about the artist's desire to return to a state of anonymity. That is, to become anonymous not as one whose name is lost but as one who desires anonymity for the sake of art. But this is only talk. The cult of personality is so strong today that whether the artist is Leonardo da Vinci or Marcel Duchamp, his work (whether the "Mona Lisa" or the "Mona Lisa" retouched with a moustache) is seen first as an object connected with the artist's name and his legend, and only second, if at all, as a work of art with something to say, or nothing to say.

The cultivation of anonymity, even if it would be a healthy sign, would still be a kind of reverse snobbism at a time when art's connection with life is so artificial that it must feed on other values than its service to a necessity. Our only naturally anonymous artists are the commercial ones who get their jobs because they are sound workmen, whose names must not compete with the advertised product and need not be remembered except as a source of supply while they live.

A comparable position, in a society that offered them a

more significant creative field, must have been held by most of the men who supplied sculpture for the medieval cathedrals. But if you are a sculptor today, assembling crushed automobile parts to supply no other demand than the stimulation of the cocktail audience, you have to have a name and a legend (which can be whipped up overnight in the right quarters) if your stuff is not to be recognizable for what it is—temporarily resuscitated junk.

And even if you are a much better artist, a sculptor dealing with ideas instead of gimmicks, the name and the legend are still imperative, since there are no more cathedrals or temples and not many buildings of any kind that require sculpture, but only the collector and the museum to keep the artist alive in the iron lung of a patronage that is incidental to the things we really live by in our century.

This unhappy position of the artist, a position that fails to nourish him spiritually even when it does not starve him to death physically, can reduce him to the role of either decorator and stuntsman or futile introvert. He is asked to satisfy too little; too few demands are put on him by the customer; there is not enough for him to do, and so he either plays at being an artist, or deludes himself with high-flown rationalizations as to the importance of his art.

The highest-flown rationalization to come to my attention in some time is the statement by Grace Hartigan, one of the least anonymous members of the New York School, accompanying her large, typical work in an exhibition called "Art in Progress" at Finch College. The painting is a proficiently slashing, splashing concoction of color, complete with dribbles—a superior and vigorous example of its type, a type that thousands and tens of thousands of art students across the country learned, to their current sorrow, to bat out dur-

GRACE HARTIGAN: *Jolie,* 1963. 78¾″ x 57″. Oil on canvas.
Collection of Dr. and Mrs. S. Elliott Harris, Baltimore.
Photograph courtesy of Martha Jackson Gallery, New York.

ing the years when abstract expressionism seemed to be the sure thing.

Miss Hartigan's painting could be labeled "Birth," "Death," "Growth," "Blank," "Sensations in Space," "Comatosis," "Rising," "Falling," "Air," "Earth," or anything you choose. Once you have passed beyond pure incredulity, you do not know whether to laugh or cry at the earnestness of Miss Hartigan's statement that "my best work comes when I place myself in an internal state of maximum danger and anxiety . . . I am close to the primitive idea of art (magic ritual) although much of my form has evolved from the Western Renaissance tradition . . . My protest (if that is the correct word) in these paintings is against the depersonalization of sex."

Such an interpretation on the part of the artist, when the painting has no possible way of saying the same thing to the observer, except with the assistance of words, if even then— is a reduction to absurdity of the romantic idea of the artist as a peculiarly sensitive spirit who opens his sensitivities to others as a path toward spiritual increase. Great romantic art achieves this goal, but in the art of Miss Hartigan— serving here as a whipping girl—a supreme arrogance crossed with a supreme innocence adds up to nothing more than a supreme pointlessness. I'm afraid I don't feel very sorry for her. However difficult the position of the artist may be, it is only compounded when semi-artists like Miss Hartigan carry on in such a way.

March 21, 1965

Young Italians, Indeed!

Just exactly why I was foolish enough to think that "Young Italians," a new exhibition at the Jewish Museum that opened last week to run all summer, might offer something both solid and fresh, I'm sure I don't know. Pure old-fashioned association of ideas with words, I suppose—"young" suggesting freshness, and "Italians" reminding you that some pretty wonderful things have happened on that peninsula over the centuries. "Young Italians," indeed. It is just another obvious show dominated by fashions thin in the first place and now mostly on the wane, stuff we are already getting tired of because it never offered much substance although it still poses as "vital" and, God help us all, "avant-garde."

Any man still in full possession of his senses should have remembered that exhibitions of this kind are never exploratory, that whatever they include that has not already been given the full treatment in New York is going to be chosen on the premise that the more closely it is allied to something recently touted, the better. Irrationally I had hoped that somebody might have gone to the trouble of an Italian trip to ferret out whatever original talent is expressing itself on that fertile soil. Surely there is *something* original going on there. Surely not *all* talent is smothered under the weight of the international art magazines with their promotional articles posing as criticism and the international sales conventions posing as art biennials.

But nobody explores. Exploring is too much trouble. It takes too unbiased an eye, and bias is always more comfortable than the vulnerable state of receptiveness. Additionally, you are safe in exhibiting "new" art only after it has been given the promotional treatment and has become familiar to a second-string in-group.

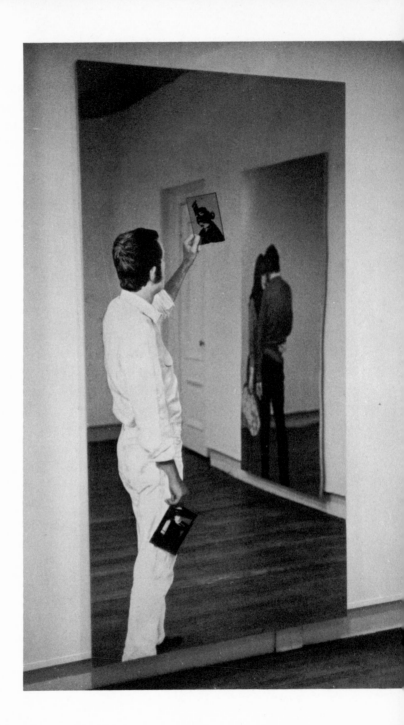

"Young Italians" offers a perfect example of cliché posing as invention in the work of Sergio Lombardo. Mr. Lombardo starts out with a sure thing among inflated blue chips, the recent rainbow arcs of Frank Stella, and doubles his bet by turning them into folding sculptures that lie on the floor and lean against the wall. It is curious that virtual plagiarism of this kind can pass for invention among the group of critics and museum people who organize such shows. Here the basis for inclusion would seem, irrefutably, to be that young Italy is most vital when it most closely imitates middle-aging America.

It occurs to me that being avant-garde today means being unable to see beyond the end of your nose. If you cannot see beyond the end of your nose, you figure that there is nothing out there (or to either side of you) and that hence you must, surely, be ahead of everyone else. I do not know whether or not Alan Solomon, who selected this show, went to Italy to do the job, but if he did, somebody wasted money. It could have been selected from promotional publications hardly less accessible than the telephone directory.

While I am fussing, I want to object to Mr. Solomon's (and his ilk's) way of making something complicated out of something simple. Now, the closest thing to a truly inventive talent in the show belongs to Michelangelo Pistoletto,

MICHELANGELO PISTOLETTO: *Man Looking at Negative,* 1967. 90½" x 47¼". Harry N. Abrams Family Collection, New York. Photograph courtesy of Kornblee Gallery, New York. The foreground figure is a life-size modified photograph and is applied to a stainless steel mirror, shown here hanging on a gallery wall. Everything "behind" the foreground figure is a reflection in the mirror, including the embracing couple, which is likewise a modified photographic image (*Self-Portrait with Soutzka*).

who applies life-size photographic figures against stainless-steel mirrors. Thus you can see your own reflection behind the figures, and the reflection of anything else, often in motion, that happens to be within the mirror's range. This is an entertaining gimmick, deftly executed, and that is the end of it. Why does it have to mean that Mr. Pistoletto "brings together that pervading Italian preoccupation with the interplay between exact location and indeterminate displacement of the surface plane, and a process of specific recording of precise things as they are in snapshot intimations of reality, using clear isolated images both of people caught in action and of objects held in stasis, like a broom propped against a wall." The broom appears on one of Mr. Pistoletto's mirrors in the show, but where did that particular "pervading Italian preoccupation" come from? I never heard of it before, and can't find anyone who ever has.

I am aware, of course, that if Mr. Solomon ever bothers to read anything I write, he finds it even more irritating than I find a passage like the one just quoted, but I object to that kind of gas less because it irritates me personally than because it is precisely the kind that gives modern art a bad name. It turns some people away because it makes them feel that they are not bright enough to play the game, and turns others away because it proves to them, quite correctly, that they are too bright to want to fool around with such nonsense. This produces that large segment of modern art's audience with no interest in art but only in something called keeping up. I would rather see great art offered to people in the form of pap—after all, its greatness remains undiminished no matter how much pap is extracted from it—than see entertaining but essentially trivial art like Mr. Pistoletto's offered to them in quasi-philosophical, pseudo-historical terms that can only emphasize its limitations at the cost of obscuring its virtues.

June 2, 1968

This Way to the Big Erotic Art Show

The exhibition called "Erotic Art" at the Sidney Janis Gallery has come and, in effect, has gone, leaving behind it no sensation more vivid than the faint, stale stirring of the air following a mass yawn. Such is the situation, at any rate, on the day after the opening, when this is being written. And although people may line up to see the show, enfevered by the promise of forbidden delights served up with intellectual sanction, the only thing that can happen, surely, is that the yawn will spread.

The show, upon its announcement during the summer, became a *cause célèbre* in advance, in anticipation of censorship. It represented, for a segment of truculent painters and writers, a chip on the shoulder that the police were dared to knock off. It was reviewed in detail before it opened, before it was even installed, by several titillated critics. They were the fortunate ones: it all sounded so lively in prospect.

"Erotic Art" was not completely installed when I saw it, either. The missing bits included the nudie movies incorporated with some of the exhibits. These weren't working, and I am told that they never did work very well, that like the movies filmed for stag parties, they suffered from amateurish manufacture and projection. But I did not mind missing them, having passed through my Blue Period at the age when fraternity bull sessions still offer exploratory charms. In truth, the exclusion of visitors under the age of eighteen has eliminated virtually the entire audience that might find some stimulation—let's not say satisfaction—in "Erotic Art."

The artists represented in the show and the usually astute dealer who staged it failed to recognize a primary truth about eroticism, which is that the pictorial description of genitalia, the representation of intercourse, either normal or perverse, and all the rest of the physical and visual paraphernalia of sex, are not erotic per se. The mere picturization of such things and such acts has nothing more to do with the erotic impulse than a photograph of an airplane has to do with the principles of flight. The great erotic works of art were not created first of all to be erotic, or at least not to be merely erotic, and the most erotic painting I know is Ingres' "Jupiter and Thetis," in spite of the fact that the artist intended it as a classically pure interpretation of a passage in the *Iliad* that has nothing at all to do with a sexual bout.

"Erotic Art" shows us a few of these bouts and is also generous in its explicit anatomical displays, but it falls so flat that it is difficult to characterize except as what it is not. It is neither a good, dirty romp nor a sophisticated display of perversion, neither a celebration of the natural physical pleasures of love-making nor a catalogue of its refinements. It winds up as a collection of objects resembling painting and sculpture by people whose names are familiar to us as the names of artists, but whose claims to the title never looked weaker.

Exhibited in an essentially non-art context, the majority of the exhibitors show that without the attendant rigamarole of pseudo-aesthetic explanations that inflate their reputations, their talents collapse and are revealed as paltry. This is a personal inconvenience for me, since, tired of complaining about everything, I had almost convinced myself that Jim Dine and Tom Wesselmann, for instance, were artists. They don't look it in this show although they are represented with typical work. I only hope that when they have their next shows I can fool myself again into thinking they have something, after all.

Mr. Janis, I am afraid, did not assemble an art show, but a freak show that fails to deliver. I could not figure out whether, as the opening drew near, the gallery hoped for a police closing, with its attendant publicity (this was the dominant presumption up and down the Avenue), or had begun to fear legal action on the chance that (witness *Eros* magazine) really serious penalties might be incurred. But if the gallery should be closed, and if I were called onto the stand to give an opinion as to whether or not the show was obscene, I think I would have to say that it was more silly than nasty. The intention of at least a couple of the artists was, I think, to court censorship in order to serve a conspicuous martyrdom. (Just a little tiny martyrdom, of course— nothing worse than thirty days in jail at most.) But what the intentions of the serious artists were, is hard to say. Aesthetic intentions are obscured by the fact that anything exhibited aggressively as an erotic object is temporarily deformed as an art object. And although the title of the show remains "Erotic Art," nobody is going to be lured into it by that little three-letter word. The fact that they are not going to find anything very erotic, either, makes this the most pointless major show in some time.

Unless, of course, it sells.

October 9, 1966

Jan Lebenstein and the Mysterious Visitors

Jan Lebenstein, a Polish painter who lives in Paris, is holding his first one-man show in this country and has filled the Galerie Chalette with a congress of "Axial Figures" (individually identified by numbers only) suggesting the priests of some lunar sect dedicated to the deity Rorschach. Ranged as if engaged in some static ritual and standing as high as eight feet, they confront you in quiet ranks along the walls, staring with doughnut-shaped eyes, presenting splayed-open pelvises like giant moths spreading their wings, and offering for inspection their rib boxes like paired ladders.

Their spines resemble the cores of giant trees, with branch-like projections that might be sensitized tentacles or receptive antennae. Here and there, their garments or their flesh (if they can be said to have either) are emblazoned with cabalistic insignia rising like heavy embroidery, like welts, or like gleaming scar tissue, and some are possessed of central orifices that might be umbilici designed as outlets for oracular messages.

The measure of Mr. Lebenstein's success is that his art, which could be only spooky, is genuinely apparitional, and that a succession of figures that might be expected to bore by repetition fascinates, instead, by variety. In addition, the elaborately ornamental character of these large panels, which have aesthetic relationships to stained glass, mosaics, enamels or metalwork, does not exist only for its own sake but is primarily an expressive force.

The curious shapes and axial symmetries of Mr. Lebenstein's figures hint that he might have begun them by applying a certain amount of pigment to his canvas, folding it face inward, opening it, and inventing from there. Actually he builds from preliminary sketches which, often Rorschach-

JAN LEBENSTEIN: *Axial Figure 111,* 1961. 90½" x 39½". Oil on canvas. Photograph courtesy of Galerie Chalette, New York.

like in suggestion, are subjected to studied elaborations.

Like so much contemporary painting, Mr. Lebenstein's, by the time he finishes it, is as close to low relief sculpture as to what we used to call painting. Gobbets and threads of paint are built up and interwoven to rise in glistening mounds, nests, and cables from the surrounding flat. This flat itself is usually eventful—roughened, stained, and freckled with bits of paint, although on occasion it may be a pure, slick black.

Transparent pigments are glazed across many of the textured areas, which may include metallic paints. The tarnished golds and blackened silvers that dominate some of the schemes, and the rigid frontality of the figures, account for frequent comparisons to Byzantine icons. But others are painted in tans and browns, in grays and sooty creams. One figure stands against a field of deep crimson. Another, the color of mist, is spread wide against a paler mist.

Polish associations as well as echoes of Byzantine opulence have inspired critics to deduce a family tree for figures that are obviously of distinguished lineage. Madeleine Challette-Lejwa summarizes some of them in her catalogue introduction, including ". . . the skeletal crucifixes of the Polish country roads . . . or the shadow of charred bodies from the Warsaw Ghetto. Others see the wrath of sinister, primordial, man-eating gods, or bellies bloated with famine, or the Kafkian vision of man metamorphosed into bug."

Such a variety of interpretations may be connected with the Rorschach relatives of the figures Mr. Lebenstein creates. In spite of the definitions he imposes on vague beginnings, he develops a mystery so personal that one is still left largely to one's own responses.

Since this is true, the critic is unsafe if he makes an interpretation, thus leaving himself open to analysis by amateur psychiatrists. But for me (taking a chance), the Axial Figures are insistently suggestive of ceremonials—of the participants, of their robes, and of their moon-changed equivalents of chasubles, miters, and reliquaries.

The artist himself has given a different explanation. He once answered a question as to what his art means by saying, "I paint man from the inside out."

This statement can be given a literal interpretation, since skeletons and viscera are suggested in the structures of the figures. But since this would make the goal absurd, Mr. Lebenstein's phrase could be interpreted as "painting the inner man." But that is not much good either.

There are forms of art that are diminished by specific definition, by efforts to outguess the artist or to counterguess other observers. Abstract art is the summation of these futilities when one tries to make of it more than an exercise in pure aesthetics, and Mr. Lebenstein is said to regard himself as an abstract painter. He is not. He is the inventor of a race of creatures who could hardly be more concrete in spite of their unfamiliarity. They disturb, they delight, they hypnotize because they are at once so tangible, so explicit, and so strange.

They have very much the attraction in this way that the art of savages and primitive peoples has when we first meet it. Anthropologists may explain it in their way, and aestheticians may analyze it in theirs, but its force remains in its evocation of mysteries we have forgotten or have buried so deeply within our consciousness that we do not know they are there.

Similarly it seems to me that Mr. Lebenstein is a kind of occultist who has materialized a band of spirits that we have known somewhere and that each of us remembers in a different way. His art is not to be explained but to be enjoyed for the responses it stimulates.

We may be specific about the secondary rewards he offers us—color, decorative elegance, technical ingenuity. These are the standard rewards in the sterile field of contemporary painting. But Mr. Lebenstein also offers evocations of the kind that, as an intimate form of communication between artist and observer, is strongest when least susceptible to wordy translation.*

April 1, 1962

* These comments on Jan Lebenstein must be taken as pertinent only to what has become his early period, since he has abandoned his "Axial Figures" for representations of human or humanoid beings engaged in the investigation of morbid pleasures. This article, however, is of particular interest to me since it is my only one to have inspired a favorable comment from Alfred H. Barr, Jr. (at that time Director of the Museum Collections at the Museum of Modern Art, and not too pleased with me), who took the trouble to send me a note saying that he found it "admirable."

Julius Bissier, the German painter (of French extraction), is sixty-eight years old.* But it was only three years ago with a retrospective at the Kestner-Gesellschaft in Hanover that he came into anything like wide attention. The exhibition was successful enough to reduce Bissier, a retiring man, to a state near collapse, but he remained next to unknown in America until last September, when he won a special Tenth Anniversary Jubilee award at the São Paulo Bienal. His first American one-man show is currently at the Lefebre Gallery.

There is not another painter anywhere of exactly Bissier's stamp. He might be called a combination of Corot and Klee for immediate purposes of description, but he should not be thought of as a synthesis or a derivation from any sources. Bissier is pure Bissier.

If you are content to find in painting no quality other than delectation, Bissier offers delectation in such abundance as to make him completely satisfying without searching for deeper values. His pictures, simply as color exquisitely applied in fetchingly arranged shapes, are, at the very least, the most expert and elegant decorations. He plays muted vermilions, soft grape-purples, and clearer blues and greens against filmy backgrounds that may turn opalescent here and there. A few clustered spots of bright color, sometimes including a patch of gold leaf, may complete a composition that is held within the uneven borders of what appears to be a scrap of canvas or paper. His typical pictures are either about seven by nine inches, or about twice those dimensions. They suggest pages torn from notebooks, or from some latter-day illuminated manuscript.

* Bissier died in 1965 at the age of seventy-two.

JULIUS BISSIER: *14. August 60K,* 1960.
7½″ x 8⅝″. Tempera and oil on canvas.
Collection of Marion Lefebre, New York.

The shapes within these small areas often resemble bottles
or vases. An occasional shadowy bit of architecture—a
two-story house, a twin-towered cathedral—may also appear along with letters, wandering lines, circles, squares,
and other patterns, all of which may be regarded either as
purely decorative motifs, or as symbols.

With symbolism we enter the region where Bissier may
be more than an enchanting miniaturist. For himself, his

jars, bottles and vases are the vessel of life; the clusters of color may be seeds, sometimes held between two podlike forms; a cathedral is part of a picture called "Dark Whitsunday" (some paintings are titled, some not); there are male and female symbols, although not with the explicit biological references of, say, Miró; the letters are sometimes the initials of friends, persons connected in his mind with the conception of the picture; there are musical references.

The puzzle in Bissier's work is why this symbolism, so personal and not apparent until it is explained, somehow manages, nevertheless, to relay to the uninitiated observer a sense that if exact meanings are hidden, there is nothing casual about these placements of shapes and colors, nothing decoratively arbitrary about their combination. The sense is one of peace, of silence, and of contemplation.

Corot, in his figure studies, relays a parallel mood through his own pictorial motifs, which are the realistic ones of a model who seems casually posed in the studio. The emanation of contemplative order (like the emanation from a Bissier) is inexplicable since, in other hands, a painting may have all the characteristics of a Corot except this single intangible one. Corot and Bissier have in common the poetic quality of gentle introspection without morbidity.

In reporting from São Paulo two months ago after a first acquaintance with Bissier's art, I said that he had "learned to cook in a school where Paul Klee was the master chef, but he follows no recipes and never repeats a dish, his own or anyone else's." This still holds, especially in the comment that no two Bissiers are alike in spite of their remarkable unity of mood and their limited and repetitious catalogue of pictorial elements. As for the comparison with Klee, it remains appropriate in that Klee, also, was often a painter of symbols in a technique and a format approaching the miniature illumination. And in both painters a superficial childlikeness, an apparently naive directness, can be the carrier for the most subtle adult allusions.

But where Klee's childlikeness may be sly, impish, and even perverse, remaining a spicy ingredient in our continued enjoyment of his pictures, Bissier's is apparent only at the first moments of acquaintance, and then dissolves like a mist rubbed away from a glass. Klee's maturity is intellectual and sophisticated; Bissier's is emotional and is, in the end, an achieved simplicity.

As a painter who enlarges and intensifies our experience, as well as one who delights us, Bissier can stand outside movements and influences. But he is further arresting as an artist who has run counter to the contemporary conventions of athleticism, giantism, and chanciness that have been propounded as the only logical expressive means for an artist in this part of the twentieth century. Historically, with his imminent emergence as a major figure, Bissier may mark a turning point by proving that intimacy, subtlety, and gentleness need not mean lack of strength; he might show us that contemplation is more important than braggadocio. And even if he does not, he has already demonstrated that delight concentrated into an area the size of the page of a book may be more rewarding than excitement inflated to the size of a wall.

November 12, 1961

Juan Genovés: Violence and Anonymity

Juan Genovés was born in Valencia, Spain, in 1930 and now lives in Madrid. Much better known in Europe than in this country, he nevertheless sells immediately anything he exhibits here. Yet he remains relatively obscure—"relatively" considering that he is one of the strongest, most immediately effective painters at work just now.

Perhaps the explanation is that his very strength and the very immediacy of the impact of his pictures puts him outside the area of chitchat where we hear most about painting today. His theme is not one that makes bright conversation at a cocktail party. He shows man harassed and hunted down by war machines (the shadows of flocks of bombers sweep across a field as flat as and less eventful than a board, where men scatter in flight, pointless because there is no protection anywhere), or by criminals (a minuscule body lies solitary in a vast, featureless space, while two tiny figures crouch and run), or by the unnamed murderous force in "Man Alone" that spotlights its victim as he twists and runs through an empty world and at last is eliminated.

There are other pictures, not many, that are more specific: in "The Prisoner" a man with his hands shackled behind his back is led by two captors down an infinite vista, from nowhere to nowhere, as if in an endless walk toward execution. In "Face to the Wall" a man and a woman, hands raised, seem to await the shots of the firing squad while in an adjacent frame they flee, perhaps a helpless dream of escape.

But Genovés is most moving when his subjects are most generalized: it is the anonymity of "Man Alone" and of each of the hundreds of little men in the terrified mobs that

JUAN GENOVÉS: *Man Alone,* 1967.
47″ x 52″. Oil on canvas.
Collection of Mr. and Mrs. Manuel Seff.
Photograph courtesy of Marlborough-Gerson Gallery.

affects us—because, for whatever reason, it is with these anonymous figures that this artist makes us identify ourselves.

Genovés uses very little color anywhere, and virtually none in his figures, which are black and gray with here and there a hint of sepia. His relation to the news photograph—his sources in it, and his independence from it at the same time—is the first key to the vividness of his style. The limitation of news photographs, even the most affecting of them —like Robert Capa's of a Spanish rifleman at the instant of death—is that we never quite lose consciousness that this is a miraculously recorded instant, that this was a real man, was a real place, was a set of circumstances at a certain instant. Everything is specific, but the word is "was." All photographs, after your first glance, enter the past tense. The more specific the record, the more it removes us from the immediate participation that we can feel in the face of a generality. We may be stirred by a photograph, but we are stirred in retrospect.

By approximating elements of the look of news photographs, even to the blurring of hasty focus, the elimination of detail by coarse printing on poor paper, and the striations that come from radio transmission (and whether this is the artist's intention I do not know, but it is the effect, which is what counts), Genovés calls on a set of vivifying associations that include, also, newsreels and on-the-scene television reportage. But by identifying no time, no place, no individual (all his men are faceless) he replaces "this was" with "this is."

I know nothing of this artist's life—whether or not he has more acquaintance with social violence than is normal to any man born in 1930, or what his sociological and political convictions may be. Whatever they are, they are not

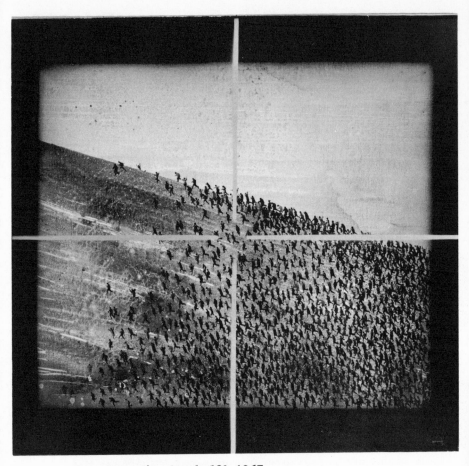

JUAN GENOVÉS: *Angulo 18°*, 1967.
55⅛" x 59". Acrylic and oil on canvas.
Collection of the Art Institute of Chicago.

obtrusive, and this is a second explanation of his power in a field where so many artists fail. Flag waving and flag dirtying are the two poles of failure for artists who, however passionate their involvement, are more likely to impress observers by their exhibitionism than by their argument. Beginning with a sincere declamation on a problem, they usually end by saying, "Look at me!"

A strong discipline in Genovés's technique corresponds with the enforced anonymity of his actors. There is never an exhibitionistic trick; there is a deliberate reserve, even a cultivation of uniformity. The hundreds of little figures who charge and stream through his pictures are (apparently) painted from a few stencils, with minor variations added. He organizes these anonymous masses brilliantly, which is not the same thing as flashily. It is this artistry, held in check at just the right point, that immunizes Genovés from the rant, the bathos, and the paranoia that—alas for its admirable intentions—infect socially conscious art today.

"Protest art" must all but inevitably fall victim to its own intensity in the service of one cause or another. Genovés is not thus self-hamstrung. When Goya created his "Horrors of War," he was first inspired by the Napoleonic invasions, and his murderers and torturers are shown as Napoleonic soldiers. But in the end he was not telling us of a single invasion, or even about war, but about man's capacity for beastliness. In the same way, Genovés's final comment, no matter what his point of departure, is concerned with no specific protest, but with an objective comment on twentieth-century man's capacity for self-destruction.

November 5, 1967

Edward Hopper, Antaeus, and the
Loneliness of a Long-Distance Runner

At the age of eighty-two and a height of six-foot-four plus, Edward Hopper (the subject of a retrospective exhibition at the Whitney Museum of American Art) is a rangy, big-boned man whose appearance suggests that he might have been a member of his college crew around the year 1900.* Nothing suggests the wiry compactness of the long-distance runner, but a long-distance runner is what Edward Hopper has always been. His steady pace does not decrease from year to year, although today he is so far ahead of the field that you would think he might slow down a little. The best of his American competitors have hardly got their second wind and are not yet in sight behind him, and his only international competitor is Pablo Picasso. But in the race that Hopper is running, Picasso is disqualified because he has covered so much of the distance by flying trapeze.

Hopper is strictly an earth man. Like another giant, Antaeus, who was the son of Mother Earth herself, he seems to draw renewed strength every time his heel strikes the ground. And the secret of his miraculous staying power is indeed that this is a contact he has never lost.

But as a twentieth-century man, Hopper has had to go Antaeus one better by surmounting a difficulty that the primeval Titan never had to face. Much of Hopper's long course has been run through Metropolis; he has painted New York with as much perception as he has painted Cape Cod. And he has demonstrated his capacity to draw his earthy strength through the insulating layer of asphalt and concrete that has forced most contemporary artists to synthesize their energies from artificial ingredients.

* Edward Hopper died in 1967 at the age of eighty-five.

EDWARD HOPPER: *Hotel Room,* 1931.
59½" x 65". Oil on canvas.
From the Nate B. and Frances Spingold Collection, New York.

Hopper's earthiness, however, has nothing to do with rusticity, coarseness, or even heartiness and good humor. He is earthy only in the sense that he is of this world, and his special power is that he sees this world with an extraordinary combination of objectivity and interpretative response.

In the face of nature, or what is left of it, Hopper always checks himself well this side of lyricism and reminds us— for instance, by showing us the roadside gasoline pump in front of a pine forest—that nature in an urbanized century is only a relative concept. He can paint, as few painters can, the purity of the sky, the freshness of morning near the sea, the soft clarity of the light that strikes across dunes or grass and onto white clapboards. But nature is never an ineffable mystery for Hopper; he has no interest in the ineffable—or at least, by the evidence, he does not regard painting as a medium for expression of the ineffable. Nature for him is reduced in scale by the presence of men, by their cottages and lighthouses. The people who sit on porches or by open windows are warmed by the sun and refreshed by the air but are inspired to no philosophical ponderings.

By giving us a picture, Hopper supplies us with this selection of raw material for such ponderings if we want to make them for ourselves, but he does not dictate their direction. He is an extremely reserved artist. His apparent objectivity is in truth a kind of fastidiousness, an unwillingness to intrude because he does not want to be intruded upon. He establishes in each painting the common ground where he is willing to meet us, and expects a mutual respect of its limits. He sets these limits by employing motifs so insistently prosaic, and by representing them with such apparent di-

rectness, that it would be easy to think of his art as nothing
more than communication by description.

But of course it is the nature of the description that makes
the difference. In the deepest tradition of realism, Hopper
describes by selection and emphasis, so that while he seems
to be telling us nothing more than what everybody already
knows, he is constantly demonstrating that nothing need be

EDWARD HOPPER: *New York Movie,* 1939.
32¼″ x 40⅛″. Oil on canvas.
Collection of the Museum of Modern Art, New York.

prosaic except as our habits of seeing and thinking make it so. His pictures say again and again that the world we call prosaic is the one that means most (partly, perhaps, just because there is so much of it) and that if we cannot understand it, then all the furbelows, exoticisms, and inventions that are also a part of the world become nothing but trivial amusements. The most inventive superstructure is of no account unless the foundation is firm, and every foundation is tied of necessity to the earth.

But the earth is increasingly encased in a rind of concrete, and its dominant natural features are no longer trees and hills but buildings. It has subways for caves and sewer gratings instead of springs. Hopper paints this aspect of nature with even greater power than he does the remnants of nature as it used to be. No other painter has caught the city's hard, flat, night light in quite his way, and no other has quite realized, as he has, that the sun, when its light cuts into the city in the early hours, is an ancient foreign eye that shows us streets and buildings with a disquieting revelation of their spiritual threat.

But just as Hopper finds nature reduced in scale by the presence of man, so he finds the city warmed by the persistent humanity of its anonymous inhabitants. Somehow they manage to be not quite defeated without even knowing that they are in battle against a dehumanizing force. Hopper's city people sitting at the all-night lunch stand, his apartment dwellers reading their newspapers in cramped, barren rooms, his plain-bodied girls dressing in the morning, his usherette trapped in the cheap, plushy gloom of the movie palace—all these people, as subjects for a painter, are vulnerable to sentimental or condescending treatment, but Hopper treats them with a respect that dignifies them not through any effort to exaggerate their importance—for individually they have none—or to give them a sweetness they do not possess, but by recognizing the right of human beings to exist, and by respecting their right to whatever inner privacy they may maintain as the last fortress against the assault of mass living.

It is this respect, this apparent refusal to pry beneath surfaces, that gives Hopper's cityscapes the quality of poetry disguised as objectivity, the crux of his art. He can paint the ugly, mechanical face of a tenement with its blinds drawn and make us aware that the individuals filed within the cubbyholes are sentient beings.

But at the base of Hopper's respectful and even loving perception of the world, especially the city-world, there is a loneliness so complete, so fully accepted as inevitable, that it is hardly poignant. The isolation of the people who sit side by side at the lunch counter, of the men reading their newspapers and a girl dressing or undressing within a few feet of someone else who is doing the same thing on the other side of a thin wall, and of the usherette and the members of the audience, in gray twilight breathing and rebreathing the same air, yet beyond hailing distance of one another—all exist in an isolation tolerable only because it is the natural state of things.

Hopper is a lonely painter and the painter of loneliness. Only nominally connectible with any school or movement (with, for instance, only the most tenuous connection with the genre and social realist American painting of the 1930's), he has made the long run alone, without tripping over an ism or going off course into the blind alleys that so many of his generation mistook for new goals. He must have been sustained by the same spirit that saves his paintings from sadness in spite of their recognition of the human dilemma: the conviction, at bottom, that the sum of all the prosaic bits of the world adds up to life, and that life in its sum is meaningful.

This is a contention easy to dispute, but Edward Hopper is not the artist to dispute it with.

October 4, 1964

Venice on the Potomac

Would you be interested maybe in a delayed report on a recent fiasco? If so, I am in an excellent position to deliver it, having just returned from a wintry visit to Washington, D.C., in lieu of Venice last summer, to inspect the American section of the Biennale as installed in the National Collection of Fine Arts.

I wish, by the way, that a Citizens' Commitee would get together in Washington and tell the taxi drivers where the National Collection of Fine Arts is. They always deliver you triumphantly to the front door of the National Gallery, even though you have entered the cab at the airport protesting that that is not where you want to go, that you want to go to the National Collection, which with the National Portrait Gallery is housed in the renovated Old Patent Office Building. The various cabbies who have shared exploratory adventures with me since the place opened had never heard of any of this, nor had any of the cabbies they hailed in traffic. This last time I got out and telephoned and have now memorized the address. The building you want is located on the city block bounded by F and G Streets and 8th and 9th Streets, N.W. or S.W., I forget which. Just now, however, there is no urgent reason for you to make the trip.

I am sorry to have to agree with the majority opinion that the group of American paintings and sculptures chosen by Norman A. Geske, of the University of Nebraska, who served as commissioner-at-large for the sponsoring Smithsonian Institution, make a disappointing show. I still insist, however, that the letdown does not negate a point that has been inadequately recognized, that Mr. Geske's premise in selecting the figurative tradition in recent American art as his theme was not only valid by historical record as well as immediately contemporary assumptions, but was courageous as well. He could much more easily have turned out a glittery show acceptable to the influential group who occupy themselves between Biennales by prefabricating and packaging merchandise for the next one.

Mr. Geske's selection offers us five painters and five sculptors who represent a cross section (or rather, as the first difficulty, only certain spots of a cross section) of the most complicated and most deeply rooted aspect of American art. Analyzed, a selection that lacks character when it confronts you in the gallery makes sense on paper and should have bred a winner instead of a flop:

First, let's take a couple of grand old men as the major figures, candidates for the international award. Let them be artists who as young men were obedient to European standards (primarily the School of Paris) but who have resolved their problems in an American crisis. Who, then, but the painter Edwin Dickinson, the *Grande Liaison* between academy and avant-garde in America, a lyrical classicist, in tandem with a fervent expressionist, Reuben Nakian, who has achieved a comparable position among sculptors?

Next, let's pair a painter and a sculptor of the next younger generation who have served as spokesmen for figurative art among colleagues who all but unanimously, among the most vivid talents, adopted abstraction. Obviously this means Richard Diebenkorn, representing the San Francisco Bay area painters, a man who played a historic role when he renounced non-objective painting in 1955, and Leonard Baskin, who has "assumed all the risks of a dedicated polemicist" and whose "commanding skill has given currency to his arguments on behalf of man and society during a period that has made a cult of disengagement." (The quotes are Mr. Geske's.)

Then, just to dispel any lingering impression that figurative art is primarily concerned with the world we see, let's have a painter whose visual legerdemain puts the commonplace into the service of disquieting introspection, and a sculptor whose respect for the figurative tradition does not exclude "a convoluted, mysterious, and evocative concern with self-understanding"—respectively James McGarrell and Robert Cremean.

Pop art, as an explosive figurative rebellion, must be recognized in a contemporary figurative show, but (partly because pop has already had its day in the Biennale) only in pop-related manifestations. The sculptor Frank Gallo, who has sent pop's satiric commentary to the beauty parlor and the finishing school, where it took an art appreciation course in Renaissance styles, fills the bill here, along with

FRANK GALLO: *Girl on Couch,* 1967.
48″ x 51″ x 40″. Epoxy.
Photograph courtesy of Graham Gallery, New York.

the painter Byron Burford, whose inclusion is possibly explicable on the score that it is a good idea to introduce a minor reputation to spice a list of well known names.

Finally, a painter and a sculptor whose work projects them more as personalities than as artists and whose contrast indicates the range of temperament attracted to figurative art in America—the bland, patrician Fairfield Porter. with his Ivy League version of the impressionist-intimist tradition, and great big bouncing Red Grooms, the All-American bumpkin.

There are at least four names on this list that I would never have included, but there would be at least that many on any other list attempting to cover such ground, so I see no point in quarreling. The point is that even if we grant the possibility of an ideal list, I suspect that the show would have been equally dull. For that is what it is—dull. And the sad thing is that it is dull because it is good; it is good because of its variety and yet monotony seems inherent in it.

The differences between these artists are often extreme but they cannot be made apparent to the casual observer by the simple device of juxtaposition, and art exhibitions of the Biennale kind must be geared to excite the visitor, not to make him think about anything. In the opposing camp, the camp that objected to Mr. Geske's choice of figurative painting as reactionary, you have no such difficulties. You can juxtapose Helen Frankenthaler—all great big swirly runny areas of decorator colors—and Ellsworth Kelly—all great big bright slick cleanly cut enamel samples—to immediate dramatic effect because their differences are explicit and obvious within the tiny conceptual range that they share.

No matter that it is only momentary drama, immediately

exhausted. Momentary drama is all you need—but oh, how you do need it for these big international shows! Miss Frankenthaler and Mr. Kelly are painters bred by and for transient dramatic exhibition. Without liking either of them very much, I must admit that I have enjoyed their kind of exhibition more than I did Mr. Geske's in Washington. Still water may run deep but, dammit, it's awfully still.

Perhaps, too, there were too many artists in the show. Except for Mr. Dickinson, with the star spot, and Mr. Nakian, with too much space for so repetitious a group of sculptures, everyone seemed cramped within the limitation of four works each. We had samplings rather than summaries. On the other hand, perhaps one example each by seventy artists might have yielded a better (let's use the awful word and say more exciting) show than seventy examples divided among ten—but that wouldn't have supplied a candidate for a Biennale award.

Leonard Baskin suffers under a special difficulty as the exhibition is installed in Washington. His alcove is contiguous to that of Red Grooms, who has incorporated tapes of old jazz records in his "Chicago" environment. Although I am on record several times over as an admirer of Mr. Baskin's strengths as a sculptor, and for a much longer time have been a fan of early jazz, I found it impossible to split my personality on this occasion between Mr. Baskin's bronze "Achilles Mourning the Death of Patroclus" and Mr. Grooms's "Lonesome Mama Blues."

It was Mr. Grooms who carried the day, and in truth he carries the show, which is the saddest comment on the nature of these shows in spite of the fact that Mr. Grooms turns out some delightful and exhilarating inventions. His "Chicago" combines the allures of a cheap carnival midway, a Punch

and Judy show, raucous satire, and high-spirited documentation of Chicago's rough, tough, legend of raw vigor devoted to corruption, all in the spirit of the 1920's and 1930's, which is odd, since Mr. Grooms wasn't born until 1937, when it was all running down. To bring the Washington exhibition up to the moment, he has added a panel about the recent Chicago violences, but it doesn't amount to much. What Mr. Grooms is really interested in is fun, and he can not only take it, he can dish it out. (That is a 1930's reference, if you don't recognize it.)

January 5, 1969

"F-111" and the Day the House Caught Fire

"F-111" is a series of fifty-one panels adding up to a length of more than 85 feet, painted by James Rosenquist, that appears to be an effort to bring pop art of age. The Metropolitan Museum is an institution nearly a hundred years old, directed by Thomas P. F. Hoving, that to date has been dedicated to the exhibition and preservation of works of fine art. Currently "F-111" is on exhibition in the Metropolitan. I am of two minds about the whole thing. Sometimes I think "F-111" comes off worse than the museum does. At other times, I think the museum comes off worse than "F-111" does.

RED GROOMS: *Chicago,* 1968.
Photograph by George Tames, *The New York Times.*

JAMES ROSENQUIST: *F-111* (partial view), 1965.
10′ x 86′. Oil on canvas and polished aluminum panels.
At left are the owners, Mr. and Mrs. Robert C. Scull.
Photographed at the Metropolitan Museum of Art
by William E. Sauro, *The New York Times*.

As an ex-painter of the kind of gigantic signs that urge us to see this or that movie on Times Square, Mr. Rosenquist, a charter member of the American pop art group, has held from the beginning an indisputable claim to legitimacy. Where his less fortunately trained colleagues had to synthesize styles reflecting the vulgarities of the American scene upon which pop art capitalizes, Mr. Rosenquist's sign painting was triumphantly vulgar to begin with. His bumptious awfulness has been his strength.

The weakness of "F-111" is that Mr. Rosenquist, or somebody acting as his mentor, decided that bumptiousness was not enough, that it was time Mr. Rosenquist turned out a Social Document with a Program. "F-111" is it. Named after the fighter-bomber of the same initial and number, "F-111" is an assemblage of billboard-size billboard-style illustrations of industrial-military aspects of our society, from light bulbs to the hydrogen bomb. A visual double entendre shows a mess of spaghetti with tomato sauce that might be human entrails—this, at least, is my interpretation of the passage. The climactic panel shows a little girl under a hair dryer that could be the nose cone of a space missile, a double comment (as I see it) first on the cultural perversion that takes little girls into beauty shops and then on the misalliance of science and barbarism by which the same little girls may be atomized.

JAMES ROSENQUIST: *F-111,* detail.
Collection of Mr. and Mrs. Robert C. Scull, New York.
Photograph courtesy of Leo Castelli Gallery, New York.

This one panel shows that "F-111" could have been a good thing overall. Standing alone, it is at least a wry if not powerful comment—a sick epigram of sorts. But it cannot carry the rest of the panels, where the point is not extended but only belabored, and belabored feebly at that.

A fundamental trouble with "F-111" as a social comment is that it negates its reason for being: although it is full of sinister prophecies of the end of our world, it says at the same time that our world is so hideous that we might as well blow it up and be done with it. But to worry about whether or not "F-111" has a reason for being is to take it too seriously. Pretentious and juvenile in conception, Mr. Rosenquist's great big pseudo-editorial is not too bad when it is taken as an entry in the vaudeville sweepstakes of the international exhibitions where it has been prominently exhibited. At the Metropolitan, on the other hand, where our standards are lifted the minute we enter the doors, "F-111" becomes an embarrassing exposure. How weary its photomontage approach to composition; how stale its pretensions to literacy; how flat its declamation; how unprofitable its effort to invest the agreeable highjinks of pop art with sober meaning. Pop art in "F-111" takes up where Salon art died a well-deserved death almost a hundred years ago. It is an outsize picture aspiring to eloquence but ending in fustian, successful in one ambition alone, the ambition to occupy a large amount of wall space in a prestigious institution.

The Metropolitan has been stirred to take Poussin's "Rape of the Sabines," David's "Death of Socrates," and a variation of Leutze's "Washington Crossing the Delaware" from their places in other galleries and has hung them with "F-111" under the title "History Painting—Various Aspects." Even "Washington Crossing the Delaware" deserves better than this, and the other two paintings are simply sold into prostitution. A coherent exhibition of aspects of history painting could very well conclude with "F-111," but the Metropolitan's slapdash, last-minute effort to justify a lapse from policy is difficult to stomach.

Or perhaps it is not a lapse from policy. Perhaps it is symptomatic of new policy, which would make things even worse. We are assured that Mr. Hoving is engaged in the admirable program that he outlined when he assumed the directorship, and in that promise we must put our faith. But while great projects are gestating, we are being treated to rather trying evidence of a taste for stuntsmanship that seems to have been acquired while he was doing a good job as Park Commissioner. He made a beautiful transition from the cloistered Metropolitan to the limelight of that job, but now that he is back, he seems to miss the excitement. He needs another transition.

The museum's announcement of its discovery that its famous Greek horse was a fake was made in the museum's auditorium with flourishes unequaled by anything since the first time a woman was sawed in half on a public stage, and one almost feels, upon entering the Great Hall nowadays, that one must check to see whether a bicycle rental stand has been installed by the sales counter and whether the Grand Staircase has been turned into a ski slope. Either innovation would be more welcome than a departure made in connection with the exhibition of "F-111," when Robert C. Scull, who with Mrs. Scull owns the painting, was invited to expound his ideas in a fireside chat for the museum's Bulletin, supplanting the curators and other scholars who normally contribute to that publication.

These comments, of course, are made from this writer's judgment that "F-111" is not a painting up to the Metropolitan's standards, and his feeling that surely Mr. Hoving knows it isn't. That is not fair to Mr. Hoving, since he has stated that he finds "F-111" to be of timely sociological importance—but such a conviction on his part is in itself distressing. There seems to be no way out.

Except, of course, that there is always the rest of that wonderful place, the Metropolitan Museum of Art, to wander around in. Just forget that we made any objections.

February 25, 1968

Among readers who did not "just forget that we made any objections" was Mr. Hoving himself. He in turn made public objections, and as a result the above article was followed by this sequel three weeks later, published under the title "The Day the House Caught Fire" after I had reluctantly given up the one I preferred, which was "Don't Tread on *Me*, Buddy!"

Among themselves, critics recognize a code of professional ethics by which, from time to time, it is permissible to relax by writing something called a think piece. This is a privilege that I have often enjoyed, but it looks as if those days are over. An aspersion on the quality of my thinking, cast from a very high place a couple of weeks ago (a rostrum in Buffalo occupied for the evening by Thomas P. F. Hoving, the director of the Metropolitan Museum), has left me so self-conscious on the score of what goes on in my head that I am afraid I must give up thinking altogether as the only alternative to indulging it as a secret vice. I am already pretty well tapered off, having had the support of family and close friends who could be called on when with-drawal symptoms grew too distressing to bear alone, and I certainly do not intend to disrupt my regimen by doing any thinking here. Anyhow, the way I see it is, why should I go on breaking my back week after week? With so much non-art around, what's so wrong with a little un-think?

This week I would like to write about a friend I once had, a young woman who came home one day and found her house on fire. But first a few words about Mr. Hoving, a young man with whose welfare I feel concerned in a fatherly, even a grandfatherly, way.

I want to explain to the citizens of Buffalo about some-thing Mr. Hoving said while making the opening address at the Second Buffalo Festival of the Arts Today. When he waggled his finger and said, in the course of emphasizing the importance of dynamism as the paramount objective in museum policy, "I detect today in some quarters certain manifestations toward a type of middle-age, or even old-age, thinking," he was not admonishing the good people of Buffalo who were his hosts and his audience, but was re-ferring respectively (I take it) to my colleague Hilton Kramer, who will never see the bright side of thirty again, and myself, who edged out of first youth some years ago.

Both Mr. Kramer and I had raised objections in our columns to young Mr. Hoving's exhibition of James Rosen-quist's "F-111" in the Metropolitan, and to what we con-sidered some attendant errors of judgment. Mr. Hoving's assumption that everyone in Buffalo devours the art columns of *The New York Times* was flattering but, as it turned out, unwarranted. Without a clue to what he was talking about, his audience naturally thought he was running them down. I hope that this explanation will restore our director to the good graces of Buffalo, where, at the moment, he is thought of as having condescended to the local gentry. Next time, Mr. Hoving should just go ahead and use my name. After all, I use his.

Now for my friend whose house caught fire. As I have said, she came home one day and found it ablaze. Rushing in through the front door with the idea of saving whatever she could (there were no children or anything like that), she issued from the back door without suffering so much as a singed eyelash, but when she came to herself an hour or so later, standing across the street looking at the smoking remains of the place where she had lived, she found herself holding in one hand an egg beater from a kitchen drawer and in the other a red glass bowl from the living room table that had been a wedding present and that she had often prayed God she would break while cleaning house.

Her unhappy experience used to prompt me, over the years when I was still thinking, to think about things like this. One never knows when a similar occasion will arise, and one's obligation goes beyond selfish personal considerations to an obligation to society at large. Suppose one night very late when everyone in Paris except you has gone to bed, you are going back to your hotel on the Rue Bonaparte after an unaccustomed excursion into high life on the Right Bank, and you are cutting across from the Rue de Rivoli toward the Pont Royal, and you see an unaccustomed glow in the windows of the Louvre with curls of smoke issuing through the first red-rimmed holes in the roof. What are you going to do? Are you going to pretend you haven't seen anything, and thus get shut of that tiresome weatherbeaten old she-dragon, the "Mona Lisa," for keeps, or are you going to rush in and save something, and, if so, what?

The Louvre, I am afraid, is too big a problem, and considering the present strained state of my relations with the Metropolitan Museum, I do not think that I had better say whether, if all this were to happen at the corner of 82nd Street and Fifth Avenue, I would run first to save "F-111" or Mantegna's "Adoration of the Shepherds." But of course if Mr. Hoving were in there, I would try to save him first.

I can see it now. He has collapsed just inside the main entrance and is lying there all arms and legs, but when I bend over to put him into some kind of order for lifting, he springs to life and I get the old one-two. The next thing I know, he has carried me outside and flash bulbs are popping. Who, oh who, could have alerted the press? The pictures in the paper the next morning are very good of Mr. Hoving, but I look terrible, like a bundle of old rags, and the headlines say "Hoving Captures Museum Thief." What are we coming to, with this kind of thing going on at our greatest museum?

March 17, 1968

2

Letting Off
Steam

How Come

The following pieces were written without effort to chasten strong feelings by tactful expression, and with foreknowledge that their publication would enrage admirers of the artists in question. It did, and the admirers expressed themselves in packets of hate mail. The last piece of the group, directed not against an artist but against a synthesized correspondent called Mrs. Gumboil, also caused unease, not in the breast of Mrs. Gumboil but among well-wishers of mine who feared it might alienate a section of the public. In truth I had hoped it would, but apparently it did not, since Mrs. Gumboil's unwelcome solicitations continue to come my way.

In defense of harsh and even biased criticism, I would like to requote Peter S. Prescott and Anne Prescott, who rose to my defense in a letter to the editor some years ago after the *Times* published an attack on me signed by a group of artists, collectors, dealers, professors, and other critics who had been infuriated at my stepping on some of their best-loved toes. Whether or not Mr. and Mrs. Prescott would respond favorably to the articles included here I do not know, but this passage from their earlier letter has encouraged me, ever since, to go ahead and let off steam when I feel like it:

Often, but not always, it has appeared that the more sweeping the generalization, the more forthright (or injurious) the language, the more effective the criticism. The bite, not the justice, of the commentary is often what makes it memorable, and perhaps in the long run more valuable. Consider Ben Jonson's observations on Spenser and Donne, Dryden's attack on Shadwell ("For Writing Treason and for Writing dull"), Pope's broadsides against Theobald, Cibber and Addison ("A tim'rous foe, and a suspicious friend")—this is insulting language at its best. Dryden and Pope were not just attacking their subject's professional competence; like many critics, they were wreaking a personal vengeance by slandering their motives as well, and very effective—judged by its longevity—this kind of thing is. Sam Johnson wrote most unfair and injurious essays about Cowley and the Metaphysical poets; T. S. Eliot abused Milton, and Edmund Wilson is most effectively unjust to the detective story. The value of these essays lies in the response which they provoked, and herein lies the ultimate value of good, if obstreperous criticism: its readers react strongly; they re-examine and re-evaluate the texts, canvases, and movements under attack.

I might add to this a statement by the painter-sculptor Barnett Newman in "For Impassioned Criticism"—or so it has been quoted to me—in which he urges critics not to be timorous. Since my criticism of Mr. Newman is very impassioned, we will get to him first in this group of self-indulgences.

Nix on Barnett Newman's Stations of the Cross

Give a man enough rope, they say, and he'll hang himself. The adage received double proof this week at the Guggenheim Museum. That body hanging from the rafters belongs to the painter Barnett Newman, and the companion object swinging alongside is Lawrence Alloway, the museum's curator, who wrote the catalogue for Mr. Newman's exhibition of fourteen paintings called "The Stations of the Cross."

A third casualty is the museum itself. The Guggenheim can no longer be taken quite seriously as a first-rate institution when it devotes its space to the exhibition of such pretentious yardage as Mr. Newman's "Stations of the Cross" and its money to the publication of such obscurantist verbiage as Mr. Alloway's genuflections in front of them. Since cigarette manufacturers are required to state on their packages that smoking may be hazardous to your health, it is unfair that the Guggenheim should be allowed to operate without posting a notice that its exhibitions may endanger the very standard of quality that the museum purports to uplift.

It isn't just a matter of charging fifty cents admission for a show that isn't worth a plugged nickel. Mr. Newman's show is worth a plugged nickel of anybody's money and has something of the same counterfeit nature. The trouble is that the Guggenheim authenticates by its imprint the validity of an exhibition so meretricious that within the few days since its opening it has become the object of appalled snickers along the art circuit.

One may argue that this is a matter of critical opinion and that Mr. Newman has other defenders than Mr. Alloway. And so he has. But these defenders always remind me of stuntsmen taking a lead from Mike Nichols and Elaine May.

Mr. Nichols and Miss May used to perform a wonderful act in which they asked the audience to give them a line to begin with and a line to end with, and they would improvise the connecting material in the style of any author. Mr. Newman's supporters among the word-slingers are nearly as clever: they can begin with any given premise and reach the conclusion that Barnett Newman is the greatest thing that ever happened. They fall short of Nichols and May, however, since these performers always made sense while bridging the gap.

"The Stations of the Cross" are fourteen examples of Mr. Newman's usual product, which is never subject to more than minimum variation within its acutely limited boundaries. Each canvas is six and a half feet high and five feet wide, and each consists of one or more vertical bands of black or white, like unraveled phylacteries. We might add here that Mr. Newman is not a faker. He believes in what he is doing. And so, surely, do his admirers.

Mr. Alloway's first sentence in the catalogue, and just about the last that seems supportable by the evidence of the paintings, is "Newman did not begin these paintings with the idea of The Stations in mind." If Newman had finished them without getting that idea, the exhibition would have been harmless as another of his taking-off points for pure theoretical dialectics. Newman's paintings have been invaluable in this respect, placing in their near nonexistence no limits upon their interpretation. But when they are called "The Stations of the Cross," you really can't make it work.

Mr. Newman doesn't make it work. Mr. Alloway doesn't

BARNETT NEWMAN: *The Voice*, 1950.
8′ x 9′. Egg tempera and enamel on canvas.
Sidney and Harriet Janis Collection gift
to the Museum of Modern Art, New York.

make it work. The catalogue's royal Easter purple jacket
doesn't make it work. And not even the Guggenheim's
cachet can make it work. A museum can give legitimacy by
proxy to just so much nonsense and no more. There comes
a point when we must admit that the nonsense can de-
legitimize the museum, and this has happened to the Guggenheim at last.

April 23, 1966

Out of Patience with Robert Motherwell

In getting Robert Motherwell off our chest, let's not try to be too polite about things. For a sympathetic evaluation of his contribution to American art you may read the Museum of Modern Art's catalogue of his current exhibition of paintings and collages, or you may go directly to the documents where Mr. Motherwell himself, in great heaving masses of words, has expounded his significance. It is a curious thing that the mention of Mr. Motherwell's name always triggers, through a conditioned reflex, the comment, "He's so articulate." The people who keep saying that should go to the dictionary, where they will discover that they have been confusing the definition of "articulate" with that of "garrulous."

My only reason for landing so hard on Mr. Motherwell

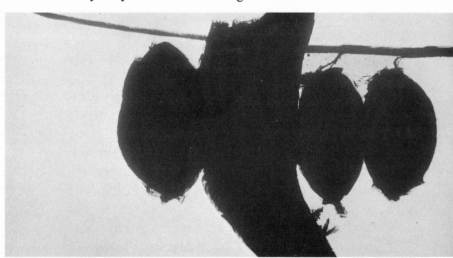

ROBERT MOTHERWELL: *Elegy to the Spanish Republic, No. 78,* 1962. 71″ x 132½″. Oil and plastic on canvas.
Yale University Art Gallery, New Haven. Gift of the artist.

(who, according to people who know him, is a charming fellow) is that he exemplifies all the weakness of abstract expressionism with none of its virtue. He has the school's basic superficiality, working from the premise, but not admitting, that painting today can be nothing better than a demonstration of the laying-on of paint. But he has none of the flair and dash that makes, for instance, de Kooning's laying-on an acceptable end in itself and even, in its limited way, expressive.

Mr. Motherwell is an extremely awkward painter, and his mammoth canvases are parasites upon their titles— "Elegy to the Spanish Republic," for instance. Who must not feel obliged to respond respectfully to something called, "Elegy to the Spanish Republic"? But the paintings are inherently meaningless, as adaptable to one title as to another, and indicate at best only Mr. Motherwell's determination to turn an amateurish ability to imitate his betters into channels more significant than theirs.

The worst thing I can say about Mr. Motherwell is that a flighty, fashionable talent like Joan Mitchell's becomes a tower of interpretative strength alongside his. He has been for a long time in the position of being accepted on his own verbal explanatory grounds, but I think it is time for his fellow painters and his colleagues among critics to stop listening, and to look at him, if they can, as if they had never seen him before. They would not see much—a really charming small collage or two in which an intelligently directed but derivative talent is fulfilled to its limit, and then some of the most flatulent acreage in the history of large-scale painting.

October 17, 1965

Yves Klein, who died in 1962 at the age of thirty-four, and whose *chef d'oeuvre* some years ago was an exhibition consisting of a gallery left totally empty, is just now the subject of an exhibition at the Jewish Museum. The probability that the show is being offered seriously as a legitimate function within the institution's program dedicated to the dissemination of positive cultural values—and surely I am not assuming too much in crediting the Jewish Museum with some such policy in spite of all the evidence to the contrary —has got me feeling peevish. Yves Klein is being touted as a prophetic artist, and in a certain awful way he was. The trouble is that the terms "prophet" and "Messiah" are being confused, as if Klein had come to us as the savior of art.

Since writing that sentence, I am thunderstruck to discover that Pierre Restany, in an introduction to the exhibition's catalogue, actually does refer to Klein's "messianic influence" that "dominates the entire present course of artistic pursuit." I had thought that I was exaggerating, with that Messiah bit. But you can't exaggerate the absurdities spoken seriously about Klein. Read on through the catalogue (better do it by degrees, for it is highly fermented) and you will come to a reference to "the prodigious exaltation of his cosmic sense."

The prodigious exaltation of nonsense is the really troubling thing about this exhibition. Only acute myopia, deliberate self-delusion, profound cynicism or a chronic case of avant-garde conformism on somebody's part can account for the museum's presenting Klein to the public as anything more than an entertainer or idea man. In these capacities he is legitimate fodder for a six-week's stand at a museum that has to compete with so many others in New York in an area where the bottom of the barrel must be scraped and re-scraped to keep new shows going for the sake of the gate. Klein was one of the best entertainers and one of the most fertile idea men in the business, but as anything more he is unacceptable.

The museum has failed to include a re-creation of Klein's masterpiece and summary prophecy, his 1958 exhibition of a void held at the emptied Galerie Iris Clert in Paris, where three thousand people (so the report goes) tried to get in on opening night to see the emptiness. More than a prophecy of what was happening in the circles where artists like Klein are taken seriously, the show was very nearly the prophecy's fulfillment. Art had vanished entirely—only stuntsmanship remained.

In a concession by which somethingness infringed upon the purity of nothingness, Klein had painted the exterior of the gallery a solid blue, known as Klein Blue, in reference to his previous nearly-nothing style in which a number of panels painted a solid eventless blue had been the entire show. (Leo Castelli favored us with a repeat of that one here in New York.) You can find Klein Blue in a tube labeled "ultramarine" or in a bottle of old-fashioned laundry bluing, if this is still being manufactured.

Klein made his own stamps (Klein Blue) as postage for the invitations to the Paris opening, and most of the envelopes went through the mail unquestioned. There is a symbolic parallel here. In a way, Klein himself, full-panoplied in cap and bells, has gone through the mail to the Jewish Museum and the other places where art is supposed to be a serious affair worth the money and time people spend on it, and has gone through on his own say-so. If he thinks he's cosmic, he's cosmic, so let's not bother to look twice. The legitimacy of what artists like this offer is not really examined because it is presented with such aggressive confidence that the enormity of the absurdity becomes its own protection. Impertinence becomes the supreme principle of aesthetics.

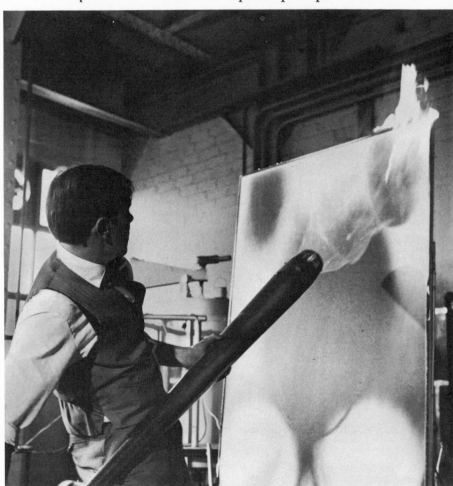

YVES KLEIN, fire-painting.
Photograph by Pierre Joly–Véra Cardot.

Klein obviously had an absolutely glorious time during his short life, popping out with one stunt after another in the great pleasure spots of the world, where somehow the pursuit of the cosmic kept leading him. But if he is a prophet he is a prophet in a very gloomy way, not at all in a way he intended or that his admirers are willing to perceive. A man of tremendous bounce and audacity—one of the truly great vaudevillians—Klein presented as liberations of the spirit a series of tricks that are more accurately interpretable as symptoms of art's mortal illness. Come to think of it, mortal illness and liberation of the spirit have a time-honored association, but I hardly think that we will get very far on that tack in this case.

Now that we've got these objections out of the way—and very graciously, too, if you ask me—we might see what the Jewish Museum is offering in the way of entertainment, which from now on will be our point of reference for the proper evaluation of the art of Yves Klein. Well, there are those famous exercises where naked girls were smeared with paint and set down or rolled around on canvases. These are called "Ants," short for Anthropometry, and while not very amusing in themselves, do supply raw material for fantasizing. They also supplied material for a movie, which I have not seen.

Then there are the sponge sculptures, which are mostly sponges stuck on wire stalks, and tinted. As an idea for the kindergarten this would supply a lot of those objects of the kind that children bring home and you have to keep on display until they forget about them, but it is hardly an idea that would be acceptable to even the feeblest artsy-craftsy magazines with the lowest standards of design and performance.

Then there are the most successful things, fire paintings. These are panels that have been burnt with resultant patterns of smoke, charring, and other disturbances. Some of them are quite handsome, but just where the hand of the artist is important here is a mystery, nor are these creations possible subjects for the philosophical interpretations that have been grafted onto them.

But where are we getting? Overall, the exhibition is about as entertaining as an old scrapbook with, for instance, the paper hat you saved from that party that was so much fun. If you want to see what a party it was, and what a handsome chap Yves Klein was, the catalogue is full of glamorous pictures, including a final bang-up profile accompanied by, God help us all, a little page about how Yves Klein isn't dead really, because people keep seeing him around here and there. I am not exactly sure what this is all about or whether I should believe my eyes, but there, like the rest of the Klein cult, it is.

February 5, 1967

Our National Pride: The World's Worst Sculpture

The latest issue of *National Sculpture Review,* the quarterly publication of the National Sculpture Society, has just reached this desk. Any issue of that publication is always good for a bitter laugh or two, but the current one is no joking matter. It is devoted to the World War II memorials that were given over to the busy chisels of sculptors blessed by the society, and it is an altogether appalling document. If our military tactics had paralleled the absurdity with

DONALD DE LUE: *Spirit of American Youth.*
St. Laurent-sur-Mer, France. Photograph courtesy of the
American Battle Monuments Commission, Washington, D.C.

which the National Sculpture Society has memorialized our battles, the GI's would have landed on the beaches in rowboats and wearing hoop skirts.

It isn't just that the sculpture is old-fashioned. The trouble is, it's just plain bad. At best innocuous, it becomes offensive when its stale, trite, and altogether specious idealism is compared with the bloody tragedy it supposedly commemorates. These memorials do not say "Remember." They do not even say "Forget." They simply give no sign of awareness that anything at all ever happened. The agony of the men who died need not be commemorated for itself, since the accepted function of war memorials is to distill an expression of an ideal from the bestiality employed in defending it. But the living men who create war memorials, men who were lucky enough not to get drowned, shot, burned alive, or disemboweled, have no right to fold their hands over their paunches, so comfortably intact, and say, "It was all pretty glorious, and when you come down to it, downright pretty." That is what these memorials say.

The irony of these tea-party monuments is that they have been created, to use the term loosely, at a time when American sculpture is more vigorous than it has ever been before. There are dozens of American sculptors today, working in a wide range of styles, who could abstract from even a secondhand knowledge of war, and from some elementary concept of what war means as a social institution, monuments that would be aesthetically satisfying and in some way related to the subject. God knows I am not an unqualified admirer of the stuck-togethers of Richard Stankiewicz, the American leader of the international group of sculptors who weld discarded machine parts and other junk into something like sculpture. But a mammoth tower of wrecked planes, rusted LST's (Landing Ship Tanks, if you have forgotten) and twisted girders, rising against the sky, could have a majesty and would evoke the sacrifice that the National Sculpture Society thinks of in terms of spun sugar.

How the commissions can have fallen with such dreadful consistency to the least imaginative, most sterile, aesthetically most tightly hidebound and reactionary stone-hackers at work today in this country would be a mystery if the National Sculpture Society were not widely reputed to have one of the most effective lobbies in Washington. The society's name suggests that it is a Federal agency—the NSS. Of course it isn't, but as things have been working, it might just as well be an arm of the American Battle Monuments Commission, which is.

Founded in 1898, the National Sculpture Society stated certain of its aims thus in its certificate of incorporation:

"To spread the knowledge of good sculpture; foster the taste for, and encourage the production of, ideal sculpture for the household and museums; promote the decoration of public and other buildings, squares and parks with sculpture of a high class; improve the quality of the sculptor's art as applied to industries and provide from time to time for exhibitions of sculpture and objects of industrial art in which sculpture enters."

That is fine, but it is only words. If you can bear those words in mind, or if you care to reread them, let us compare them with this reverse paraphrase, a sufficiently sympathetic statement of the goals of the National Sculpture Society by the evidence at hand:

"To stifle good sculpture; to foster the taste for, and encourage the production of, quasi-ideal sculpture for the aesthetically illiterate household and the atrophied museum;

BRUCE MOORE: *Female Figure*. Honolulu, Hawaii. Photograph courtesy of the American Battle Monuments Commission.

WHEELER WILLIAMS: *Airman*. Cambridge, England. Photograph courtesy of the American Battle Monuments Commission.

ALBINO MANCA: *Eagle*. Battery Park, New York City.
Photograph courtesy of the
American Battle Monuments Commission.

promote the disfigurement of public and other buildings, squares and parks with sculpture of 'high class,' with every implication of that term as synonymous with slick vulgarity." Being unfamiliar with the society's activities in the field of industrial art, I cannot paraphrase the last section of its declaration of aims, but it would seem plausible that Albino Manca's eagle in Battery Park, dedicated in 1963 to memorialize 4,596 men drowned in Atlantic coastal waters, could be an "object of industrial art in which sculpture enters"—an old radiator cap designed in the thirties and rejected by Detroit.

When the first American World War II memorials began to appear early in the nineteen-fifties, they were blasted (only verbally, alas) in a way that would have made less atrophied sculptors or a less atrophied American Battle Monuments Commission take a second look at their handiwork. But the most recent monuments follow the same style, a style that was never anything but modish and became demodé long before the war opened. The Honolulu memorial to the men who died in the Pacific and Korea was completed last year and is not yet dedicated, but Bruce Moore's bosomy Liberty girl who adorns it, all 30 feet of her, is only the female counterpart of Wheeler Williams's inane effigies on one of the earliest, and still most offensive, memorials, in Cambridge, England. And speaking of atrophy, there is Donald de Lue's "Spirit of American Youth," near Omaha Beach. Having got away with this in 1956, he did it again last year and called it "The Rocket Thrower" for Flushing Meadows.

The architecture embellished by these puerile disasters is in keeping with them—blocky, antiseptic wastes of marble suggesting the forms so dear to Hitler and Mussolini but without the sheer, brutal weightiness that made those monuments perversely impressive. Effeminated by the same kind of good taste dear to the National Sculpture Society, this architectural style might be identified as Fascist Louis XVI.

At a time when the Federal Government increasingly professes interest in the arts, the most convincing evidence that this interest is genuine would be to rein the influences that, having produced this lamentable succession of offenses to valor, are still busily cornering other commissions for public works of art.

July 25, 1965

Goodby, Mrs. Gumboil

The mailbag of anyone who is allotted a column in *The New York Times* includes hundreds of communications that are very nearly identical. Hence it occurs to me that an answer form can serve one and all of this repetitious group. Time and energy will be saved, and irritation avoided, if this composite response to some standard queries is filed for reference:

Dear Mrs. Gumboil:

Thank you very much indeed for your very good letter of the nth inst., and especially for your introductory paragraph in which you say such very kind things about what I write. I am delighted to have pleased.

Now for your second paragraph.

I do regret very much that I cannot visit your husband's studio to see his work with the idea of devoting a Sunday column to the discovery of a major artist, but we have a regulation about that. Practical considerations force us to use our limited space for the discussion of such minor artists as have come to the attention of such institutions as the Museum of Modern Art, the Whitney Museum of American Art, now and then the Guggenheim, and some of those commercial galleries who have so consistently turned your husband down. I know that this is really tough on him in spite of his acquaintance with the Van Gogh syndrome, which proves that the turned-down artist is always the good one.

One thing I would like to suggest, though, is that you abandon the term "dedicated artist" when soliciting attention to your husband's work. I have no doubt that your husband is dedicated or that he thinks of himself as an artist, but "dedicated artist" has unpleasant associations—at least it does for me.

What I have never understood is why no wife ever writes me telling me that her husband is a dedicated businessman and that I should give him a little business for that reason. Frankly, Mrs. Gumboil, it makes no difference to me whether an artist is dedicated or not. All I care about is whether he is any good. "Dedicated artist" has come to mean, to me, an artist who is not good enough to make the grade but sticks to the dreary task of being dedicated anyway. It is odd that no one would expect me to buy stock in the firm of a dedicated businessman who has demonstrated his incapacity to run a business profitably in spite of his dedication, while everyone, or at least every wife of an unsuccessful artist, thinks that I should be charitable to the dedicated artist who is no good in spite of his dedication.

I suspect that the majority of good artists are dedicated to their profession, but I am sure that there are many good ones who are just plain talented, which is better, and who knock out some pretty good things in an undedicated spirit. Frankly, when I hear an artist called "dedicated" I always remember how, when I was in high school, I was always being urged to make a date with some very plain cornstarch-pudding-type girl because she was "sincere." Know what I mean?

Parenthetically, let me suggest also that you abandon the ploy of calling the office or of having your friends call the office to engage in a conversation that runs like this from your end:

"Hello, is this the art department? Well I just had to call to tell you that I've just been to this art exhibition at the Obskew Gallery and I saw this painting by an artist, I forget his name, but I was so excited I just had to call right away. I think the name was Adrian Gumboil, something like that. Yes, that was it, Adrian Gumboil. Adrian Gumboil, G-u-m-b-o-i-l. Anyway, it was a perfectly strange name to me, but this man's a genius. I was really bowled over by this Adrian Gumboil's painting, and so was everybody else in the gallery—they were all standing around talking about how wonderful it was. I was simply bowled over. Obskew Gallery, XXXX Madison Avenue, and really I think if you went around there you'd have a real find, none of this crazy stuff you always hate, but something really wonderful like you are always hoping for. I have no idea who he is. I just thought I'd call, because I really think you'd have a real find . . ."

I'll remember the name. Now for your third paragraph.

No, I do not think that the painting that has been in your family's possession since 1880 is Leonardo da Vinci's original sketch for "The Last Supper." Leonardo is not known to have worked in Crayola on shirt cardboard, for one thing.

As for the other painting, in oil, showing a bulldog wearing a pink bow on its collar and being fondled by a small girl-child, and signed with a signature that looks like "Brxowf," I am unable to identify it from your description and am unwilling to hazard a guess as to its value. I suggest that you take the matter up with the Parke-Bernet Galleries or, if they are not alert to the painting's market potential, with the Metropolitan Museum. In either case, and I say this confidentially, you might do better not to mention my name.

Fourth:

No, please do not bother to send me examples of your fourteen-year-old daughter's drawings for an estimate of her talent. Her complexion will probably clear up in the natural course of things to make way for the practice of other talents, and the whole art question will become academic.

In conclusion, going back to the question of your dedicated husband, I note with interest your statement that this self-effacing man does not know that you have written me about his work, and that "he would be simply furious if he knew, and would probably shoot me dead."

In that case, if you are sure, let's tell him. Shall we?

Respectfully,

J. C.

January 3, 1965

3

*The More or Less
Recent Past, or Far Away
and Long Ago in the
Twentieth Century*

Pascin and a Fact of Life

Julius Mordecai Pincas, who shifted the letters of "Pincas" to "Pascin" and painted under that name, was born in 1885 in Vidin, Bulgaria, became an American citizen in 1920, and died in Paris in 1930, a suicide by hanging, after writing on the wall, in his own blood, an apology to his mistress: "Pardon, Lucy." He had always claimed that by the age of forty-five an artist has said whatever he has to say (a contention not borne out by history). In his own case, the artist had also lived just about all that he could live.

At forty-five, Pascin was paying the conventional pre-penicillin price for a sexual life that had been initiated precociously in a Bucharest bordello (or perhaps earlier when he was at school in Vienna) and had been continued enthusiastically in Paris and elsewhere. He was probably suffering, in addition, from cirrhosis of the liver. He was, at any rate, suffering, and depressed, and forty-five years old.

His last New York exhibition, at Knoedler Galleries that same year, had received unfavorable reviews, but any distress that this caused him should have been countered by his new contract with the French dealer Bernheim-Jeune. Pascin threw away the large advance, typically, on parties that amounted to open house for anyone connected with the arts in Paris. (These parties were especially popular with the hungrier set in Montparnasse and Montmartre.) Max Eastman, in a memory of Pascin written for the catalogue of the

103

current Pascin retrospective at the Whitney Museum of American Art, remembers that at one of Pascin's parties in a large apartment ("his own I assume") the decorations included "besides static ornaments, two beautiful and naked maidens nicely placed on a couch against the wall as one might place flowers in a vase."

The simile is apt, and could very nearly be extended to Pascin's typical paintings of nude or half-nude girls and young women where, although every bit of the canvas breathes a powdery, scented and languorous sexuality, the flesh and the rumpled, gauzy bits of underclothing are painted in tints and textures appropriate to blossoms. As a technical master, Pascin is a twentieth-century stylist, with his gossamer touch and his hypersensitive line (lines like nerves define the contours of nacreous thighs and breasts). But as an expressive artist he belongs less to his century with its interest in formal abstractions than to the eighteenth-century tradition of erotic sensibility—the tradition that began with Watteau in poetic reverie, was turned by Boucher into big business, degraded by Greuze as a mawkish per-version and recognized by Fragonard as the first delightful fact of life, to be treated sportively or with tenderness as the occasion dictated.

It is a French tradition, even more specifically a Parisian tradition, and in spite of his origin and his adopted citizen-ship Pascin was a thoroughly Parisian artist. He shares, in varying admixtures, the sensibilities of his predecessors, even, on occasion, the dreaminess of Watteau. And in the best of his drawings he has something of Watteau's power to represent the weight and texture of relaxed flesh with nota-tions that could seem cursory at a glance but are final descrip-

JULES PASCIN: *Anne Harvey, 1929.*
21¾" x 16¾". Pencil.
Collection of Mr. and Mrs. Bob London, Atlanta, Georgia.
Photograph courtesy of Perls Galleries, New York.

tions. The mood is not Watteau-esque; nevertheless there is an insistent mood of detachment on the part of the models (even when the reverie edges into mere boredom) that saves Pascin's sexuality from the expensive vulgarity of Boucher's or the simpering allure that in Greuze masked a nasty mind.

There is never any question but that Pascin, like Boucher, is aware of his models as sexual prospects or sexual souvenirs. Frequently, too, there are perverse suggestions, a fetor barely detectable beneath the perfume, a fascination with innocence debauched. But Pascin is never suggestive. He never snickers. And like Fragonard, he can be tender without falling into the trap of sentimentalism.

Like so many other artists who have found an insistently personal style and stuck to it, Pascin is seldom thought of in terms of his early work. He found himself through contradictory inspirations. There exist some raucous satires from his days as a cartoonist in Munich, numbers of ribald drawings full of bounce, a few testimonials to his admiration for Matisse, and an extended record of his experiments with cubism.

But Pascin could not make a cubist of himself. He had little feeling for the analytical basis of that revolution. With great facility he turned out pseudo-cubist patterns tinted with delectable hues that reveal no connection with formal structure—if ever they were supposed to have had any. Pascin found his true inspiration, as a technician, one step further back in art history: he found it in Cézanne.

But neither did he see Cézanne as an artist who struggled with the problem of structure. In the delicate washes of the watercolors, Pascin found the source of his iridescent scrubs. One thinks of Fragonard again, not because Fragonard ever painted in this manner, but because the delicacy, the verve, the control, and the unquenchable freshness are qualities shared if differently produced, and (which is the important part) are qualities that fuse with the subjects to make exquisite personal expressions of what might have been banal vulgarities.

May 28, 1967

The Germanness of Max Beckmann

Among the two hundred paintings, drawings, and prints in the Max Beckmann show at the Museum of Modern Art there are twenty-seven self-portraits. In these he reveals himself through his face and bearing as a German in three foreign countries during three periods of personal and national history—in Italy in 1907 during a brief Florentine sojourn, in 1938 in Amsterdam, after his expulsion from Germany by the Nazis, and in this country when he was at the height of his international fame.

Beckmann, by the evidence of his paintings, was an artist whose creative gift was most effectively stimulated by the spectacle of social tragedy. He matured during a cataclysmic period that saw his own prosperous country subjected to humiliation and bankruptcy by war, then lived to see the degradation of the Hitler regime, and annihilation by a second war that terminated with the world-terror of the atom bomb. Among the hundreds of artists whose lives spanned the same period, including the great art revolutionaries of the century, Beckmann is the only one who, in retrospect, seems to stand at its center to summarize it in positive terms as the appalling moral catastrophe that it was. The nihilism of dada, the morbid escapism of surrealism, the removed intellectualism or hyper-personalism of abstraction, all seem peripheral comments compared with Beckmann's. Only in individual pictures, notably in Picasso's "Guernica," can we find a comparable moral and social involvement.

Beckmann's art may be beyond national boundaries in its widest message, but his life and his art were shaped by the fact that he was a German during those years. He was the last of the great German painters to give expression to a temperamental anguish that perhaps still exists as a spiritual residue in Germany today, but which, if it exists among artists, is lying fallow. Since the debacle, German artists have been more preoccupied with capitalizing on an impersonal clarity, with great faith in mechanical precision, than in exploring the philosophical doubts and the areas of emotional stress that, until now, have been the first concerns of German artists of much stature.

As the last of the twentieth-century German expressionists, Beckmann was modern enough to have been included among Hitler's "degenerate" artists, but he is easier to tie to the philosophical broodings of Dürer and the mystical anguish of Grünewald than to the formal inventions that took over as the major expressive means of contemporary art during his lifetime.

As a German in the old tradition, Beckmann came into his own creatively when his world was demolished. His self-

MAX BECKMANN: *Self-Portrait, Florence*, 1907.
38½″ x 34⅝″. Oil on canvas.
Collection of Dr. Peter Beckmann, Oberbayern, West Germany.
Photograph courtesy of the Museum of Modern Art, New York.

MAX BECKMANN: *Self-Portrait with Horn,* 1938.
42⅛″ x 39¾″. Oil on canvas. Collection of
Dr. and Mrs. Stephan Lackner, Santa Barbara, California.
Photograph courtesy of the Museum of Modern Art, New York.

portrait of 1907, in Florence in the happy days, shows us the dapper son of a prosperous father in a world that still felt sure of itself. But Beckmann had been searching for a more intense expression than the portrait hints at, and had seemed to welcome any event that might release such an expression. After his mother died the year before, he had painted a picture called "Great Death Scene" of rather forced emotionalism, where conscious crudities and grotesque distortions are unsuccessfully theatrical rather than truly dramatic.

In 1908 he tried his hand at a big "Resurrection," where the various participants again have the air of insufficiently talented amateur actors. When the Titanic sank in 1912 he painted a huge canvas filled with capsized lifeboats and struggling figures, but managed only a superior illustration. But in 1914 as a member of the medical corps in the German army, he was transformed into an artist by emotional shock. From that time on, during the war years and the German agony that followed 1918, and climactically with the rise and triumph of Hitler, Beckmann grew as a social moralist who developed an individual style, at once coarse and brilliant, in which his special fusion of mysticism and social awareness is realized.

When Beckmann painted his own portrait in Amsterdam in 1938, the questioning man he brings face to face with us is only in a factual sense relatable to the young German who painted himself in Florence. Beckmann now sees himself as a spokesman; he would like to assume the role often attributed to Goya, "the spokesman of his time." This is an impossibly elevated position in a time so complex, but Beckmann at any rate spoke for a portion of that complexity in

his allegories of good and evil. The allegories cannot be precisely interpreted, but in their heavy forms, brilliant colors, references to war, to the theater, to vanities and to sacrifice, they play on the general theme of social violence, of the individual's capture or subjection within it, and of the hope for spiritual release.

I have always felt, in spite of efforts to feel otherwise, that after the end of the war in 1945 Beckmann became a stylist, rather than a painter who expressed himself through a style. By 1950, the man in the self-portraits is once again dapper and jaunty. The fortunate boy who painted himself in Florence has indeed become father to the man, and the paintings of the last years have a way of revealing an unwelcome degree of artifice in even the best of Beckmann. But in this best there remains an emotional record of three decades of social history not approached in the work of any other painter who witnessed it.

December 20, 1964

MAX BECKMANN: *Self-Portrait in Blue Jacket,* 1950.
55⅛" x 35⅞". Oil on canvas.
Collection of Morton D. May, St. Louis, Missouri.
Photograph courtesy of the Museum of Modern Art, New York.

Fernand Léger Is Alive and Well

Fernand Léger, who was born in 1881 and died in 1955, is an artist with an inexhaustible capacity to surprise. The fact that he surprises is the biggest surprise of all; by the rules he should be predictable. The rather bland and very repetitive nature of his subjects; the obviousness of his style, based on the simplest reductions of forms to geometrical equivalents; the seemingly primitive use of color, suggesting that he had a tube each of spectrum red, orange, yellow, green, blue, and violet and used them straight—none of this should add up to an art of much range or variety. And yet every time a new Léger show comes along, the old familiar Léger, as familiar as ever, somehow looks different. It is not so much that the art of the moment, whatever it happens to be, sets off Léger's individuality for better or worse. Rather, paintings that may be thirty or forty years old seem to absorb and reflect back to us our current vogues, as if Léger were still alive and modifying his style under their influence.

In the tandem Léger shows now at the Perls Galleries and the Saidenberg Gallery, Léger's perpetually new look is

FERNAND LÉGER: *Composition au vase de fleurs,* 1919.
12½″ x 8¾″. Pencil.
Collection of Saidenberg Gallery, New York.

doubly apparent because it takes two forms. In the paintings at Perls—just about as vivid a group of pictures, surely, as has ever hung anywhere—Léger seems to be a more elegant compatriot of some of our pop artists—for instance, of Tom Wesselmann with his "Great American Nude" series—and at the same time a more hedonistic colleague of the color abstractionists—for instance, Frank Stella with his rainbow arcs or Kenneth Noland with his stripes. In paintings such as "La Jeune Indienne," these antithetical subdivisions of painting in the 1960's are combined.

If there is anything more than a coincidental relationship between Léger and painters today, then of course it makes him either prophetic or even quite directly a road sign that these painters observed en route to their destinations. But Léger in no way seems left behind. It is as if he had tried, successfully, to capitalize on the exuberance and wit of pop art while distilling away its crassness, and to bring colorism back to its proper function as an interdependent element of painting while making the most of what the Stellas and others have managed to show us about creating maximum impact of one color field against another.

At the Saidenberg Gallery such thoughts are less likely to occur. This is an exhibition of drawings, watercolors, and gouaches, where even the brightest color is by nature of the medium softer. Also, the selection begins with a drawing of 1910 and pays considerable attention to Léger's cubism and his conversion to the mechanistic conventionalization of the 1920's, whereas the paintings at Perls, although they begin with one of 1918, are dominated by the strongly decorative, often vivacious style of the late 1930's and on.

The effect of the Saidenberg show was to convert me once more, this time perhaps for keeps, to the early Léger, an artist I have frequently questioned. The cubist watercolors, and especially a group of pencil drawings from the early 1920's in his mechanistic style, establish the solidity of Léger's position among his own contemporaries just as strongly as the late paintings reveal his unexpected brotherhood with ours.

FERNAND LÉGER: *La Jeune Indienne,* 1944.
32" x 51¼". Oil on canvas.
Collection of Perls Galleries, New York.

In spite of the fact that he was never more than a pseudo-cubist, and far from the strongest member even of the "Section d'Or," Léger adapted devices common to both of them in the invention of abstract or semi-abstract patterns of great animation and unexpected delicacy, even charm. And the mechanistic drawings, in contrast with the corresponding paintings, which can date pretty badly, are evidence of a disciplined effort to apply to pictorial art the ideal of architectural purity that he picked up from his friend Le Corbusier.

And yet the better he is, the more Léger makes me wonder just how much of an artist he was in the sense of one who develops and applies a set of procedures to achieve a self-imposed goal, and just how much he was the opposite, an inspired primitive. His work in whatever period, with its unyielding definition, its unequivocal declaration of choice in form and color, seems to give him the former character. But everything he wrote about art (and everything I once heard him say, in a lengthy lecture and interview) was either naive or obtuse if it wasn't secondhand. Leave out "obtuse" and the same can apply to his painting if we add the transforming element of a special sensitivity that marks the inspired primitive. Such artists (Douanier Rousseau, to make the comparison extreme) depend on familiar devices developed by other artists (in the case of Rousseau, the realistic, pseudo-idealistic representation of the academic tradition that he admired) but apply them with an innocence that, perversely, can be cultivated as a form of sophistication, once it has attained expressive momentum.

With Léger, this momentum increased right up to the end. It was marked by occasional lapses, the worst of them (if we forget his habitually admired but really disastrously amateurish films) coming in 1952, when he designed the mural panels for the United Nations assembly hall. His failure to understand the most elementary principles of relationship between scale, color, and pattern in painting and architecture seems incomprehensible on the part of an artist who studied architecture as a youth and was closely associated with Le Corbusier. But the failure was, actually, inherent in the nature of Léger's best work.

Habitually called an "architectonic" painter when that term was popular, Léger was no such thing. He does not descend from the classical-architectonic tradition of Poussin, as the French like to say (and as I daresay I have said myself). His art is improvisational in spirit; its supposed architectural balances are naively conceived, clear at a glance and as simple as a child's construction with blocks. Léger remains a living artist not because he deals with the eternal verities of classicism but because his art is inspired by an ebullience that can be quenched only in the eye of any observer who tries to stifle it under the traditions that Léger himself thought he followed. Rousseau, learning from sophisticated advisors that he was a primitive, deliberately synthesized a pseudo-primitive style on the basis of his genuine primitivisms. Léger, never conscious that he was other than an intellectual master of the School of Paris, remained an unconscious and hence a genuine primitive to the end of his life.

November 24, 1968

Gaston Lachaise: A Major Reservation, Hesitantly Offered

Artists, a few decades after their decease—anything from twenty-five to fifty years—enter an awkward age. Gaston Lachaise, who died in 1935, has reached it near the early limit. After a preliminary tour of the big Lachaise exhibition at the Whitney, followed by twenty-four hours of worrying, and then another tour, during which I still could not quite believe that an artist I had habitually admired for so long could look quite so bad, I was left with the question of how a sculptor who has been taken so seriously can have become dated so rapidly, followed immediately by the question as to whether a sculptor who has aged so disastrously can ever be taken very seriously again.

Neither question may be quite fair when stated so flatly, and both may backfire when this awkward age has passed, but how either can be avoided at the moment in the face of the Whitney's devastatingly revealing summary, I do not see. Lachaise did one superb statue, the standing woman of 1912-27 called "Elevation"—so good as to have become a cliché in histories of American art. It summarized all the best that he had to say in his obsessive glorification of swelling hips and gargantuan breasts like expanding universes, his contemporary version of that standard prehistoric fertility image, the Willendorf Venus, which is built around three big bulbs—two breasts and an abdomen.

But one statue does not make an exhibition, even though it may justify a life's work, and the large Whitney show, valuable historically, is embarrassing where it is not appalling as an exposure of an insistently vulgar and obvious talent. At a certain point, which is where he often begins, Lachaise's nudes, which once made exhibitors nervous for fear of offending, are just plain ludicrous or, when he is lucky, just plain grotesque. This would be fine, except that with what now seems a calamitous lack of humor, Lachaise intended to create symbols of elemental generative force.

The aggressive tangibility of figure sculpture makes impossible any completely detached or generic observation of these prancing females who, with such simple-minded pride, display the proofs of their sex like so many overinflated balloons ripe for puncturing. And the males are worse, with their clothing-store-dummy faces and their bodies where something seems to have gone wrong with the hormones in spite of the strong-man muscles.

There is a sharp line, with hardly any middle ground on either side, where pure sexuality shifts from the sublime to the ridiculous. Sexual attitudes have so changed over the last couple of decades, and artists have exploited them with such ingenuity, that Lachaise now trips over this line and falls without dignity on the wrong side of it. He has a kind of confusion between grossness and expressive power that nearly saves him by its innocence, but unfortunately this confusion involves a greater pretension that lays him low.

This is a hard judgment on a serious and very personal artist, and may very well be the result of a jaundice that leaves this particular observer increasingly less responsive to the American artists who seemed most adventurous during the 1930's. Lachaise, of course, was born in France and did not come to this country until 1906, when he was twenty-four. It was a time when American sculpture was starved for anything but tastefully traditional artists, a circumstance that must account for the enthusiasm with which we embraced Lachaise. My guess is that if he had stayed in France, even if he had developed there along the same lines that he did in this country, he would be more properly placed in historical perspective as a somewhat tardy art-nouveau craftsman of respectable accomplishment but secondary importance who occasionally hit close to the mark and who did one masterpiece inviolable by time.

On the theory that an artist deserves to be judged only by his best work (we try to forget that Michelangelo did the Pauline Chapel as well as the Sistine Ceiling), we might dwell upon "Elevation" and perhaps half a dozen surrounding pieces, and tactfully relegate the rest of Lachaise to the general area of period-style crafts such as Tiffany glass, where he could be a top man in a secondary bracket and could now be appreciated for his portraits and small figures much as we have begun to appreciate artists like Mucha. But at the Whitney we are dealing with a summary.

When you come down to it, Lachaise in the bulk is pure art nouveau, or rather he is art nouveau with the failing that he is not quite pure. His later drawings of women with Orientalized faces surmounting a series of obstreperous protuberances might have been done by Aubrey Beardsley in a hurry. His elaborately stylized portraits (the great one of John Marin, which hardly seems to be by the same artist, must always be an exception) are quite in the mood of *The Yellow Book*.

GASTON LACHAISE, photographed in 1944 with *Elevation*. Courtesy of the Lachaise Foundation, Boston.

After any big retrospective one tries to tie the artist to his sources, for which art nouveau will do in this case if we add the inevitable pinch of Rodin, and then to show that he was a prophet of contemporary art. In a few late pieces, Lachaise is sufficiently abstract to be connectible with, for instance, Arp. But oh, how one wishes he could have got around a little sooner to the realization that the Willendorf Venus herself is essentially abstract. But then, of course, we might not have had "Elevation," and that is unthinkable.

February 23, 1964

Marsden Hartley as a Gap-Closer

Full of the best will in the world, I have never been able to look at the painting of Marsden Hartley (1877-1943) with much more than dutiful respect. The current retrospective exhibition at the Whitney Museum of American Art does nothing to improve this unhappy situation.

The selection is representative, the space allowed is generous, and the pictures are spotted skillfully on the walls. The color, under these circumstances, is brightly effective, but the exhibition as a whole produced in me no emotion more profound than slight embarrassment—sometimes for the artist whose limitations were laid so bare, and sometimes for myself on the assumption that the virtues claimed for this major American reputation do exist and that I am neither bright enough nor sensitive enough to perceive them.

One virtue can be granted Hartley by anybody, however: he was a pioneer. At least this grant can be made by anybody who is convinced that pioneering per se is a virtue. But Hartley was one of those American pioneers who, in art, occupy so much less satisfactory a position than do the sturdy folk who, in covered wagons or in coonskin caps, explored non-aesthetic areas.

Pioneering in Hartley's case, which was typical of his generation in the United States, meant the importation of foreign avant-garde styles into the American scene rather than independent exploration on home grounds. The American art pioneers of his generation were thus reduced (although to say so is to make oneself unloved) to the position of second-stringers or country cousins.

Exactly the opposite is claimed for Hartley by Elizabeth McCausland, whose touchingly but extravagantly sympathetic introduction to the exhibition's catalogue traces this peripatetic American expatriate painter's adventures with impressionism, postimpressionism, expressionism, expressionist symbolism, fauvism, cubism, and pure abstraction until, at the end of his life, he made a spiritual as well as geographical return to his native soil (Maine, it was). There he discovered that his heart lay with "the lives of its simple fishing people." This argument I allow as a matter of courtesy without being able to follow.

Among the many manners he borrowed, expressionist devices dominated Hartley's own work, insofar as his work can be called his own, and in his last years he forsook all others. Yet he remained a yearner. Following the styles of painters whose achievement was to intensify experience by forcing to their limits every expressive distortion of drawing and color, he somehow managed to wind up an oddly emotionless artist.

Hartley's best paintings, the truly vigorous late Maine landscapes and the suave, economical still lifes of the same period, are good enough to show how badly he missed the mark the rest of the time. An artist should be given the privilege of being judged only by his successes, but on the other hand his failures should not be allowed to feed as parasites upon them.

MARSDEN HARTLEY: *Fox Island, Maine,* ca. 1937-38. 21½" x 28". Oil on canvas.
Courtesy of the Addison Gallery of American Art, Phillips Academy, Andover, Massachusetts.

Hartley's "archaic portraits," which also date from his last years, are marked by a truly objectionable forced primitivism. They are just plain bad, and we might as well stop pretending that they are anything else. And in most of his earlier experiments, or, rather, syntheses of other men's experiments, he displays a kind of hopeful innocence as if a gentle spirit, which he seems to have been, is paying homage to the vigor he admired in a school of painting dedicated to transcribing a world of triumphant violence.

I cannot see that within the gamut of European isms he cultivated, Hartley either assimilated or successfully adapted the innovations of the painters he studied. He could do a Braque-like still life in which each individual form is recognizably borrowed, yet in which relationships between the forms are shaky or non-existent.

In equally superficial derivations from Cézanne, he could paint a semi-abstract landscape as if it had been a papier-mâché model. As for the tortured lines of expressionist images, which in the proper hands can curl and knot or explode with next-to-unbearable intensity, he could reduce them to the scalloped edges of doilies or the puckered limpness of partly deflated balloons. In the middle range between such fiascos and the handful of late successes, there is the whole middle ground where nothing much is exactly wrong, yet where nothing at all is exactly right.

One may wonder, then, why the American Federation of Arts bothers to assemble so large an exhibition—which is about to go on national tour—and why the Whitney gives it a send-off. The best, and incontrovertibly good, reason is that this is a vividly historical show. As a representative of an awkward transitional age in American painting, Hartley is the perfect example. He was one of a generation who might be called the gap-closers.

The gap-closers pioneered not into the wilderness but in the opposite direction. They were the first Americans, fascinated aesthetic outlanders, who ventured into an advanced culture without the guide books that are so plentiful now that the international slack has been taken up. Not sufficiently Europeanized to absorb the sophistications they admired, the gap-closers were still sufficiently denaturalized to make impossible any vigorous indigenous development with the help of European innovations. They could hope at best for a synthesis that, as things turned out for Hartley, was consistently elusive. The success of Hartley's last pictures seems to me not so much in their Americanism, which is only coincidental, but in the discovery of a landscape that had not been subjected by his European contemporaries to their special transformations, and thus allowed freer play to a talent that was unusually hamstrung because its possessor could not get other men's paintings out of his mind's eye.

In Hartley's immediate generation Max Weber, who was three years younger, suffered less, perhaps because he worked within a more restricted field. Alfred Maurer suffered even more, perhaps because the mere nine years' difference in age—Maurer being the elder—made Maurer even more a foreigner in the lands he set out to explore. Yet the generation also included John Marin, seven years older than Hartley and, like the other three men, an alumnus of Stieglitz's "291" gallery. Subjected to much the same conditioning, he emerged with a style in which European influences were obvious but were overridden by a personal and American expressiveness.

An artist is successful to the degree that his means serve his expressive purpose, granted that his expressive purpose is of sufficient value as a starting point. As pioneers, Maurer and Hartley, and to a considerable extent Weber, spent most of their energy getting their compasses into working order, while Marin was blessed with a sense of direction that proved infallible and got him directly where he was going.

March 11, 1962

4

Four
Personalities

Grandma Moses

Grandma Moses, who died yesterday at the age of one hundred and one, was not a very good artist by the standards that prevail today, or, for that matter, by the standards that have always prevailed in art of much consequence. Her reputation was out of all proportion to her achievement aesthetically, but the wonderful thing about her was that the last word she would have thought of using about what she had done would have been "achievement," and the last word she would have used concerning her painting would have been "aesthetics." Her magic was that she knew how magical it is to be alive, and in her painted records of her life she managed to relay some of this magic to the rest of us.

It has been a popular jibe: "Grandma Moses isn't an artist, she's a corporation." But the fact that she was astutely managed, or rather that her product was astutely controlled on the market, has nothing to do with the fact that her art remained as fresh, as personal, and, above all, as true and as honest (without effort toward honesty) as if she had continued to paint only for her own delectation—which, as a matter of fact, she did.

Grandma Moses may remain in the history of painting as the representative type of many hundreds of untaught painters of the kind called primitives, or, at a closer level, Sunday painters, whose sensibilities have never developed the sophistications that shift "primitives" like Douanier

Grandma Moses, 1959.

Rousseau into another category entirely. She was a somewhat better artist, but not much better, than many others of her kind who might have come to similar prominence if, like her, they had been entrancing personalities with the wonderful sobriquet of "Grandma" and had been possessed of a beautiful, alert face that grew more beautiful and more alert as she approached the fantastic circumstance of a hundredth birthday.

But the important thing to remember about Grandma Moses is that the very factors that called attention to her as a human being—the "Grandma," the face, the great age —are counterparts of the factors that make her pictures— let us not say her art—entrancing. She was a human being who painted directly from a life that she relished from day to day. If she plumbed no esoteric depths, she warmly reflected some of the simplest and most ordinary, and hence most magical, aspects of the experience upon which all of us must rise or fall, the experience of meeting the world on the terms it presents to us.

The terms presented to Grandma Moses seem idyllically pastoral in her paintings, but this is only because she responded to these terms directly and unquestioningly. In a time when painters are befuddled both by life and by theories of life and art, Grandma Moses cannot be emulated. She can only be envied.

December 13, 1961

When James Rorimer accepted the directorship of the Metropolitan Museum, some of his friends thought he might be making a mistake. As director of The Cloisters, the museum's medieval branch, he had been in the snuggest kind of spot—a medieval scholar surrounded by medieval treasures and blessed with patrons who saw that there were funds to acquire whatever he wanted for the place. Except for actually laying the stones of the buildings (which in fact he did do at times) he had literally created The Cloisters. It seemed a shame for a man to relinquish such a fief even to become lord of the manor.

But he tremendously enjoyed his new position. On one of his first days behind his new desk he apologized to a visitor for looking out the window during the conversation. "I can't keep my eyes off Fifth Avenue," he said. And Fifth Avenue turned out to be even more to his liking than the gardens outside his tower window in Tryon Park. He relished the desk and the title of director and made no bones about it.

He could be an extremely stubborn man when his mind was set on a point. It was sometimes a point so small that to win it seemed hardly worth the energies of the man who much more casually made the famous $2,300,000 bid for "Aristotle Contemplating the Bust of Homer." He loved the theatricalism of underplaying at that moment, and obviously took the greatest satisfaction in his role of public figure. Every day, from the moment he left the door of his apartment on Park Avenue, he was conscious of that role, and savored it. He never tired of being recognized as the

James Rorimer, 1963.

director of the Metropolitan Museum, and whenever he pulled off a coup he never tired of applause.

But what might have been irritating vanity in a man who by simple good fortune had been lifted to high position was appealing in James Rorimer. The unflagging pleasure he took in the conspicuousness of his position was engaging in a man who had reached that position, and maintained it, because he was superb at his job. He could niggle over details because no detail of the operation of the Metropolitan escaped him, and because he knew that the grand gesture was permissible only as the climactic ornament of a firm structure. He would have been as great a director of a struggling Metropolitan as he was of the wealthy and powerful institution that he first inherited and then enlarged.

His coups in the way of acquisitions may have burst like fireworks when they were announced but they were the result of negotiations, often at ambassadorial levels and extending over years, that required the greatest tact combined with the most expert knowledge. Yet he was not by talent much of a diplomat. He cultivated a suave exterior, but his great strength as a museum director was the combination of his scholarship, his absolute concentration and unceasing exploration of possibilities and the practical means of realizing them, and his sense of identity with the Metropolitan Museum.

The identity remains. A large part of the Metropolitan Museum will always belong to James Rorimer.

May 12, 1966

When Fiske Kimball died a madman in 1955, he had put behind him a career that made him the dean of American museum directors. He had trained the young men who had assumed the directorships of most of the major museums in this country. Now, six years later, I want to add a postscript to the record of Fiske Kimball's career in an effort to correct a portrait that, as it now stands, is a bit out of focus. In spite of its personal nature this postscript belongs on the record because it concerns a public figure and a great one in the history of art in the United States.

Six years ago last month an intolerable situation forced Fiske Kimball's dismissal by resignation from his position. He was in his sixty-seventh year and his thirtieth as director. Seven months after his dismissal he died, in Munich, and in the fall of 1959 his biography, *Triumph on Fairmount,* by George and Mary Roberts, appeared.

As this biography tells, Fiske Kimball became the director of the Philadelphia Museum of Art when it was literally an empty shell of a building in 1925. When he was dismissed in 1955 his museum had reached its present eminence as one of the half-dozen finest in the country. He had scratched, dug, fought, bulldozed and finagled his way through social Philadelphia's tribal taboos and political Philadelphia's complex war dances to build and support an institution that depended equally upon the beneficence of the local aristocracy and appropriations from City Hall.

In addition Fiske Kimball was beset to an acute degree by all the other problems, except one, that afflict museum directors: whatever intramural intrigues affected the Philadelphia Museum of Art, none was directed against him, for he had the loyalty of his staff to an extent that was incomprehensible to anyone who had not worked with him.

Outsiders—like insiders, for that matter—were aware of Fiske Kimball's grossness of language, surprising in a man who wrote so elegantly; of his bluster and rudeness, antithetical to the idea of a museum director as a courtier to wealth and influence; of his prejudices, which were appalling; of his bull-in-a-china-shop technique in coping with situations that aroused his impatience, in contrast with the meticulous patience with fine points that made him a faultless scholar; of the aura of braggadocio, arrogance and even contempt that this physically huge man with the bristling Prussian brush of white hair and the heavy black eyebrows could exude as he entered a room, or when he sat behind his desk giving you five minutes of his time in which you supplied him with the material with which he would demolish you.

But for people who knew him, these exasperating contradictions were understandable as a part of his tremendous drive and his way of pounding relentlessly at one thing until it was finished, which made him not so much an efficient administrator as an overwhelming one. He never took no for an answer.

Professionally he gained the respectful support of the people he offended socially, and he gained something deeper than the respectful affection of the people who worked under him because he was loyal to them with the same force, energy, and concentration that marked his service to the museum. He might rebuke a curator in the presence of colleagues—at a staff meeting—in a way that was embarrassing to everyone and should have been inexcusable, but he was always forgiven, not because he was an appealing

Fiske Kimball, 1949. Bronze bust by Jo Davidson.
Courtesy of the Philadelphia Museum of Art.

man but because he was a strong one. His defects were like flotsam on the surface of a great tidal stream and, in fact, seemed to indicate its strength and direction.

But they indicated, too, the strength and direction of an ailment that led finally to the irrational behavior that forced his dismissal. Up to a certain chronological point in *Triumph on Fairmount* the factual account of Fiske Kimball's life, enlarged by appropriately selected anecdotes, can give a picture of the kind of man he was. But in 1953 it became apparent, through the erratic exaggeration of his eccentricities, that he suffered from an increasingly severe manic affliction, and at this point the book that will probably remain his standard biography blurs out of focus.

The last chapter, by objective factual account and illustrative anecdote, shows (without meaning to, since Mr. and Mrs. Roberts were Fiske Kimball's good friends) a once impressive figure reduced to pitiful absurdity. For instance:

"Fiske and Fraülein Mutherich set out for Bologna in the train. There they had to change to the Munich express. Fiske had an attack of nerves. He sat on his luggage on the platform and screamed at the people passing by, saying that Fraülein Mutherich was taking him to a madhouse. Then, as the fit wore off, he pretended to be a baby and kept calling to her, 'Mama, Mama!' "

After so baldly recounted an incident, it is probably impossible to explain to anyone who did not know him that Fiske Kimball even in a situation like this was not a pitiful figure or an absurd one. Lear, described in contemporary journalistic language, would also have seemed absurd, and the authors of *Triumph on Fairmount* could hardly shift, at the end of their account, to Shakespearean style.

Polite Philadelphia has been critical of Mr. and Mrs.

Roberts for having included the station-platform incident. I feel the other way: a more detailed account of Fiske Kimball's last terrible days could have risen above journalistic exposition to reveal his tragedy. The word "madness" has connotations of grandeur and tragedy, and Fiske Kimball was mad. He was desperate in the big house where he was left wandering alone after the death of his wife Marie—a tiny woman who collapsed under the strain of trying to cope with Fiske's gargantuan affliction. The museum that had been his creation was now a place that he could enter only as a member of the general public, and upon his appearance at the door, any of us who had any degree of control over him were on emergency call, assigned to follow him at a distance.

Three of us began spelling one another on eight-hour shifts in an effort to protect him, but he was elusive with the slyness of the maniac. Escaping us, he took to picking up young people off the streets, students carrying portfolios that might hold drawings, or giving any other hint that they might be part of a world he could share.

He lived those last months in a world where grotesque absurdities were manifestations of past grandeur. Anyone who lived with him through his last years felt as much as ever the man's stature and his power. But no one could help him. He was not a big man who became little, but a big man who entered wild places where he could not be reached.

February 12, 1961

A Bouquet for Miss Belmont

Gertrude Belmont's name has no current news value, and so far as I know never had any news value, but something about her should be on record. Hence this brief memoir. She might possibly be remembered by a handful of people who read this, but there is not much chance that she will be reading it herself, since she must have been pushing seventy, if indeed she had not left it behind her, when she indelibly established herself in my admiring affection thirty years ago.

At that time, a period of youthful delusion, I was studying painting, after a fashion, at the Yale School of the Fine Arts, and Gertrude Belmont turned up as a model. Take thirty from 1962 and you will see that this was during the Great Depression.

Among the minor local solaces produced by this major national disaster were the extraordinarily interesting people who modeled in our life drawing classes, taking the places of the miserable local conscripts whose sole qualification for the job was an ability to stand reasonably still and a willingness to do so with their clothes off. In their stead we had a succession of dancers, contortionists, circus performers, and other people with remarkable bodies who, out of work, took to posing as a stopgap. They were a dime a dozen, or, more accurately, seventy-five cents an hour, which, on the school's schedule, gave them twenty-seven dollars a week from which they had to pay their fare to New Haven and keep themselves fed and sheltered. This was less difficult in 1932 than it sounds now.

The Depression also brought into the classroom circuit numbers of professional models who ordinarily would have been kept busy in New York. Gertrude Belmont was one of these, a fantastic period piece who must have begun posing before the turn of the century and who brought to her profession even a flavor of *Scènes de la Vie de Bohème,* although she didn't go back quite that far.

Not that Miss Belmont was a Mimi or a Musetta. I have already said that she must have been around seventy, and she was skinny as a rake, with a large bony nose and a thin cap of hair dyed jet black, which she used to top off, while posing, with one or another of her collection of bedraggled headpieces running to crimson brocade and gilt tassels. She was always outrageously rouged.

For a professional model in life classes, nudity is, of course, in a double sense the natural state of things, but I have always wondered whether for Miss Belmont, at her age, the first pose in a new class didn't begin with a few moments requiring great courage. Those few moments certainly took a bit of adjustment on the part of the class. The first day, when she entered in her wrapper, all dyed hair and gilt tassels and ravaged face, you felt that some shocking mistake had been made, and when she began the pose some students had to leave the room, not exactly from embarrassment but from the shock a very young person may feel when he is forced to recognize for the first time the physical tragedy of old age.

But it took only the first pose to show that this was an absolutely superb model, and it took only a couple of days for our admiration to equal Miss Belmont's own magnificent pride in what for most models is only a job but for her was something not far short of a dedication. She would say, "I have a building in Chicago," or "I have a building in San Francisco," meaning that she had posed for sculpture on it, and she was as proud of having posed for certain painters as other people are of having studied under them.

She told us once that Robert Henri used to call her "the serpentine model" and had given that title to a picture of her. (I have always looked for it but have never located it.) Miss Belmont was no longer exactly serpentine, but she was a tightly strung arrangement of tendons over bone, very good to draw. One of the students commented, not in cruelty but in respectful recognition of an awesome phenomenon, that one of these days Miss Belmont was going to be wonderful to dissect. And in the technique of posing, surely she must never have been surpassed.

As standard procedure, models pose twenty-five minutes and rest five, and may shorten the posing period by as much as half if the pose is a difficult one. In our classes the same pose was held day after day for two or even four weeks; the strain on the model was considerable. But Miss Belmont refused to rest at the end of any twenty-five minutes. Her standard pose was fifty-five minutes with five minutes rest, and she sometimes shook her head when the monitor called "Time!" and went on to a full hour and a half. Most classes exhaust the model; Miss Belmont exhausted us.

At the end of a pose, when even the best models have usually sagged and shifted in spite of themselves, Miss Belmont seemed always to have just begun. Whatever the pose, she kept it alive. Usually the class or instructor sets the pose, but we soon learned that Miss Belmont had her own repertoire. These were pure archaeology, straight out of nineteenth-century academic studies, which means corny but classically affording the best exercises in problems of drawing anatomical structure.

The usual model resumes a pose after a rest by fitting herself back into a set of chalk marks on the model stand.

Miss Belmont scorned this kind of help. For each pose she had a little preparatory dance, a sort of rhythmic waving and stepping and bending, at the end of which she would stop in position. Sometimes it didn't "feel right," she would say, and she would go back into the dance. Once it felt right it was absolutely right, and there she was for another hour.

I knew Miss Belmont to break a pose only once, when a boy in the class made an off-color remark. She stepped off the stand, put on her wrapper, and walked out of the studio. An envoy from one of the girls' classes was sent to negotiate a truce in the ladies' room; this was arranged on the basis of an apology from the offender and a promise that the proprieties would be maintained henceforth in Miss Belmont's presence, a promise that was rigidly observed because by this time everybody knew that Gertrude Belmont was the best model in the world, and all the classes were competing for her time.

The school kept four or five models posing concurrently in different classes, and the happiest incident of Miss Belmont's sojourn at Yale occurred between her and one of these models, a local amateur whose name I forget but for whom "Miss Young" will do, since she was as fresh and dewy as Miss Belmont was dry and stringy.

Miss Young was an appealing girl, quiet and serious, and she took to coming into our class, whenever she had a moment, to watch Miss Belmont at work. She finally proposed that Miss Belmont give her a course of lessons, for which she would pay, and I think it was only then that we fully realized, from Miss Belmont's delight in a maestro-apprentice relationship, the intensity of her professionalism. She gave the lessons free, with special dispensation from the school to use the studio after hours.

Walking was my favorite relaxation at this time (among its other allures, it was inexpensive), and frequently on Sundays I would cross paths with Miss Belmont, also engaged in a brisk constitutional. She was never casually dressed. Hatted, gloved, and elaborately made up, she wore suits of rakish design and bright colors. I suspect that she made them herself, since they were more notable for eccentric features than for expert tailoring. I never saw her with a companion on these walks, and she and I would only nod in passing, without reducing speed, but we used to talk, usually about artists she had posed for, during rest periods in class.

Some years after I left school I began receiving postcards from Miss Belmont, who had found my address by some chance. She had retired, "having inherited a bit of money," and was living in Florida, and reported on one occasion that she had won first prize in the local fashion parade. She was signing herself "Mlle. Belmont" now, but on her last couple of cards she reduced this to a brief, firm, authoritative "Belmont." Eventually these communications ceased, with no explanation except the obvious one.

July 15, 1962

5

Money
Troubles

The Auction Game, or,
The Lost Innocence of Mr. Baddleigh Taken

This is the story of Mr. Baddleigh Taken and the firm of Starction's, a contraction of Standard Art Auctions. It is a true story, although the names are invented.

The protagonists must be introduced:

Starction's is one of the oldest and most respected art auction houses in the world. So much for Starction's.

Mr. Taken cannot be described so briefly. He is an American collector, new at the game, whose first purchases were made only a couple of years ago. Not quite within hailing distance of middle age, but already possessed of considerable means, he decided to enlarge his life by extending his interests seriously into culture, an admirable project. He not only began buying art but also demonstrated his public spirit by establishing a foundation to bring art scholars to his city to lecture. (The latter aspect of Mr. Taken's cultural adventures does not concern us here, since so far it has not run him into any interesting trouble.)

Mr. Taken has been busily educating himself in the subtle field of aesthetics and art history, but—with no pretensions to scholarship as yet—he is still at that stage of the game where his first faith must remain in the dependability of familiar name-products. He will buy a Renoir on faith because he knows Renoir to have been a good artist and because as a businessman he has learned that the law of supply and demand can be trusted when the supply is curtailed (Renoir is dead) and the demand is gilt-edged (museums want Renoir). But he is still a long way, for example, from knowing that if you can find a drawing indisputably from the hand of Primaticcio you have a treasure. He would not recognize such a drawing at an auction and might wonder why the bidding was so lively among dealers. But if he still has a lot to learn about art, he has learned one thing about art auctions, which is that you are a sitting duck if you expect them to operate within the most delicate nuances of good faith between buyer and seller.

That is how he got into trouble at Starction's.

A few months after he began collecting, Mr. Taken, who had yet to be taken, had every reason to believe that he could trust the combination of the names Renoir and Starction, and in this faith he bid on a pastel listed as Renoir's in the advance catalogue of a Starction auction. To his delight he got the picture, at a price somewhat above seven thousand dollars—a bargain, which should have made him suspicious in the first place, since bargains come up in art auctions hardly more frequently than hen's teeth.

But after he got his picture home his delight began to wane. He could not make it look just right, an indication that his sensibilities were already becoming dependable. He took the picture to New York for examination by an undisputed authority on impressionist painting, who said that in his opinion there was not a chance in the world that it was a real Renoir, and that he would so testify in court if asked.

Mr. Taken got in touch with Starction's. He wanted his money back, and had no doubt at all that Starction's would shoot him a refund. It seemed reasonable to him that Starction's would no more want to sell him a bad painting for a good check than that he would want to pay Starction's with a bad check for a good painting. He even thought that Starction's would be embarrassed by their faux pas.

Starction's didn't see it that way at all.

The transaction had been completed, and as far as they were concerned that was the end of it. If Mr. Taken wanted to sue the seller, that was all right with them. But by the standard terms of sale, an auction house is not the seller but only the intermediary agent between seller and buyer, with no responsibility whatsoever for attributions, authenticity, representations, faults, imperfections, inaccurate descriptions, or anything else except the mechanics of the change of hands, which Starction's had accomplished.

Mr. Taken could not understand this. He felt that the good name of a business house must depend upon guaranteed merchandise. But he had no legal means of redress. In the auction business, even at topmost levels, there are no regulations corresponding to, say, the pure food laws. And although auction houses sometimes withdraw a fake upon discovery, and sometimes make restitution to a purchaser, whether or not they do so is entirely up to them.

All of this was distressing enough to Mr. Taken, but his indignation (and amazement) mounted upon further discussion with Starction's. Starction's had not simply made an embarrassing error. When the picture came in for sale, they told him, they had held no doubts as to its authenticity, but, like Mr. Taken later on, they had begun to have their doubts while the picture was on the walls. Their opinion had become that it was probably a fake, but they had allowed it to go on the block as a Renoir anyway. The only comfort they offered Mr. Taken was their assurance that they still felt a residual hope to the extent of twenty per cent (a curious calculation) that the picture was genuine.

After all, Starction's said, fakes are difficult to distinguish from the real thing under certain circumstances. As to the signature, they said cheerfully, but to Mr. Taken's way of thinking not to much point, that if the signature was not Renoir's it had been forged with exceptional skill.

Mr. Taken was not interested in collecting examples of the forger's skill, and he wondered what disposition could be made of the picture to recoup at least a portion of its cost. And now he was truly and completely appalled by Starction's advice. It would be unwise to put the picture up for public sale right away, they cautioned him. Dealers would remember it, question so quick an attempt at resale, and murder it by grapevine. Mr. Taken was advised to get rid of the picture privately (presumably by fobbing it off on another collector as innocent as he had been before this experience) or to sit on it long enough so that its reappearance would not seem suspicious. Here Mr. Taken touched bottom, feeling that the insult of invitation to perpetuate a fraud had been added to the injury of having been the original victim.

There are various ways of reading this story. It has been told from Mr. Taken's point of view, although not with the passionate eloquence to which it inspires him. At the opposite point of view, perhaps Starction's, the argument could be that an art auction house is a different thing entirely from an art dealer, subject to none of the obligations upon which a dealer's good name depends, and that anyone unwilling to accept the risks involved and not yet an expert judge of what is offered for sale, has no business being in the auction room and must settle for licking his own wounds upon leaving the arena. From either point of view, the story of this little transaction is only the slightest footnote to a situation that is rooted in the art auction boom of the 1960's and spreads its ramifications to affect areas as diverse as the Federal tax laws and our aesthetic standards.

Just why so many people who know their ways around other businesses leave their savvy behind them when they buy art at auction is the most piquant of questions. Touchingly, it suggests a creditable delusion, an emotional conviction that the sanctified aura of art as the supreme expression of human aspiration must purify by its presence even the tarnished marts of trade. But when art becomes merchandise, the selling of it becomes a business like any other. Or, in the case of the auction houses, perhaps not quite like any other, but still a business. And it is a business immune to the degree of loyalty to aesthetic convictions that persists among the best art dealers, as well as exempt from the standards that an art dealer must observe in order to maintain his good name. These are standards that, by the nature of the auction business, can exist there only when they do not impede the main function, which is to get things sold. The seller, not the buyer, must be given the breaks.

On the face of it, the art auction (like any auction) seems to carry for the buyer a foolproof built-in guarantee of your money's worth. You sit there and somebody bids so much for something; you bid more; somebody else bids more than that; you bid again; the bids keep coming. At last your final bid wins out, and in the nature of things it would seem that by demonstration you are paying at most the highest but still legitimate dollar value of the object according to supply and demand. There is always the attractive possibility that you have a bargain because someone who didn't get to the auction will want to buy your picture for more than you paid. And you have the backlog assurance that even if you overbid just a bit, the penultimate bidder is always willing to take the picture off your hands at a slight loss.

By this view, auction prices are subject to the economic equivalent of the physical laws by which water finds its own level. But, alas, no. Art values (aesthetic and financial) do not exist in a state of nature. They are affected by a system of dams, pumps, irrigation, artificial evaporation, and cloud-seeding that make the Tennessee Valley Authority project look like a wading pool in the back yard. As a result, what seems to be happening at an auction may not be happening at all.

Let us synthesize, without too much romanticizing, an instance:

In the auction of a group of paintings owned by a Mr. Wrcxzw, a knowledgeable art lover who collects both for the pleasure of owning and the profit of selling, there is an excellent and authentic Picasso, probably the best picture in a consignment of good quality. The star of the lot, the Picasso might at a dealer's bring $60,000—with great luck, $90,000. The bidding at auction follows this line—very lively up to $60,000, then slowish. The auctioneer is at his most dramatic as the bids waver and then build up a head of steam. They reach a climactic $100,000, and then at $105,000 it is going, going and gone, apparently to one of those unidentifiable bidders who make their raises by wink-ing an eye, scratching an ear, or perhaps yawning, even when touching a sensational price.

That is what seems to have happened. Actually the Picasso never changed hands and was not really expected to. At a certain point well below $105,000 the bidding had stopped. But by prearrangement with the house, Mr.

Wrcxzw's Picasso was not to go for less than $105,000, although both he and the house knew that there was hardly a chance in the world that anyone would bid that much. This was not a matter of setting a protective minimum, announced before the auction began, with the picture withdrawn if an initial bid to that amount was not forthcoming. It was not even a matter of Mr. Wrcxzw's surmounting the last other legitimate bid with a bid of his own on which he paid the usual house commission. No money, as well as no picture, changed hands.

So what was the point?

The point was that auction sales prices are publicized all over the world, and that catalogues marked with the sales prices go into the files of art transactions kept all over the world. Mr. Wrcxzw now has a Picasso that is on record as having brought $105,000 at auction, a figure he might claim as a tax deduction by giving the picture to a museum. (In his bracket, the deduction could save him more money than the picture originally cost him.) Or there is a chance that someone might be both innocent enough and rich enough to purchase the picture at the induced figure of $105,000.

That is what Mr. Wrcxzw gets out of it. But what about the auction house? The advantage to them is that their reputation for being able to draw high prices from bidders may bring them important consignments, in a field where competition for consignments is intense. But there was a more immediate reason: Mr. Wrcxzw stipulated this individual deal as part of the conditions upon which he would consign the rest of his lot, a very desirable lot, to the house. Furthermore, the Picasso was of such quality that the announcement of its coming up at the sale would attract the kind of buyers an auction house hopes for. Attracted by the Picasso, they were present as a desirable bidding audience for the lesser, although still good, pictures.

As for the auctioneer, all good auctioneers are also good actors, and he probably had the time of his life improvising his performance after the true bids stopped coming in.

January 16 and January 23, 1966

The Vanity Racket, or, The Sad Dream World of Gordon Gullible

Gordon Gullible, a resident of the Middle West, is one of the tens of thousands of artists across this country who would like to have a New York show, and as a matter of fact he had one last year. Moreover, it was his third time around. But even Gordon's gullibility has its limits, and he is beginning to wonder just what he has been getting for his money. For Gordon is not one of the handful of artists who manage to make a connection with a serious gallery—a gallery visited by critics, collectors, museum curators and the gallery-trotting public. He is one of several hundred who show every year in the vanity galleries, where anybody who can pay the tariff can get a show of sorts.

If Gordon had known anything about the art world, he would have realized in the first place that such an exhibition carries less than no prestige.* It is true that many an ex-

* —although one art instructor in a small sectarian college wrote, in response to this article, that in her part of the country the words "New York show" were magic enough to bring her a raise no matter what the caliber of the gallery.

cellent painter cannot find a serious dealer to handle his work, but the one who resorts to a vanity gallery accepts the caste mark of the untouchable. The typical vanity gallery selects its artists on the basis of the artist's willingness to pay rather than on the quality of his work, and although some vanity galleries try to pick and choose in observing something like a minimum standard of excellence, all of them are essentially in the space rental business rather than the art business.

Gordon's case history, composite but factual except for names, runs thus:

Having made the usual tour of New York galleries toting a bundle of photographs and color slides of his work, and lugging one original under his arm, and having met with uniform rejections ("Just about the most humiliating experience you can have"), Gordon somehow remained so innocent that he failed to wonder why any gallery should advertise for artists when artists are pounding at every gallery's door. Discovering such an ad tucked away in a corner along with ads for current exhibitions, Gordon thought he had made a find, responded, and was told to send his samples to the Galeria Vanitas "for inspection." Sure enough, he made the grade by return mail.

The Galeria Vanitas charges Gordon thirty dollars per canvas for a two-weeks' show. Along with his twelve canvases in his latest show there were twenty-seven by four other artists in the gallery's two small, shabby rooms and a hallway. If the take is calculated by these figures, the Vanitas (which is always filled with a show, but always empty of visitors) brings in $2,340 a month. That is hardly big business, but the gallery's expenses are not great either —the rent for the cubbyhole in a run-down brownstone, the cost of the luring advertisement, and a little something for the modest printed announcements (described in the contract as brochures listing the works) that go to the press and the artists' friends.

The gallery does not require a staff, since in its undisturbed quiet the proprietor can do his own mailing and bookkeeping. When a visitor wanders in, he is greeted with the question "Are you a friend of the artist?" If the answer is no, the next question is "Are you an artist?" If the answer is yes, the proprietor has a bit of business to propose. When time hangs heavy on his hands, he may do a bit of dusting and repairing of the frames he keeps on hand to rent to his exhibitors.

There is nothing literally dishonest about the Vanitas, since it is frankly what it is. But its clients do not realize what it is. They think they are getting a New York show when in effect they are not. Strictly by the letter of the agreement, the Galeria Vanitas promises no more than it delivers. The contract states that "every effort" will be made to interest museum directors, collectors, and university art departments (which sometimes have jobs to offer). But since all these directors, etc. know that the Vanitas will never have anything that interests them, just what "every effort" to interest them might be is a big question. The one promising show in a thousand that might come there by a fluke is just not worth the investment in time required to visit the other 999.

"Every effort" will be made, the contract says, to obtain reviews in "the leading newspapers and art publications," but the only publications that send a runner to the Vanitas are those that make a policy of giving a few lines to every show of every kind that is announced in any gallery or so-called gallery. The kindest thing that serious reviewers can do for a Vanitas show is to leave it unmentioned and they observe this charitable policy consistently.

Finally, "every effort" is to be made to reach "as wide a buying public as possible," but the "as possible" is the catch. At the Vanitas there really is no possibility at all. Although the gallery contracts for a twenty per cent cut on sales, this is one expense the artist need not worry about. As a sidelight on the psychology of the innocents who exhibit in the vanity galleries, the prices they set on their work are likely to be higher than those of many artists of established reputation. The vanity gallery artist lives in a world of dream.

One gallery wrote Gordon Gullible that his work was "very interesting" and that the Director of Exhibits thought it would be a good idea to let the gallery hold his first show in Belgium "as a basic introduction of an American's work before bringing the show to New York." Just what is basic about Belgium as a place for an American to make his debut is a very puzzling thesis, and even Gordon was not much impressed by the ploy, although he was much impressed by the expenses involved. The Galeria Vanitas is relatively inexpensive. Other galleries with more elaborate façades and a more selective standard that makes them only semi-vanity get two or three times as much. Even so, if Gordon had had a one-man show at the Vanitas instead of showing with other artists, he could have paid up to twelve hundred dollars.

Some pathetic stories come from people who have been taken in by the shadier galleries that flourish at lower levels than the Vanitas. There was the gallery, now happily defunct, that charged a flat one hundred dollars per canvas as entry fee (and was quite firm about cash in advance) for a supposed competitive Salon with purchase prizes. The gallery was packed with pictures, their number having been increased by the gallery's foresight in limiting size to 24 by 30 inches maximum. It is a fair assumption that the purchase prizes went to planted pictures and reverted immediately to the gallery's coffers.

There was the vanity gallery director who told a prospective client, who had described his young son's work, that he was ready to give this youthful genius a show sight unseen. There is the painter who wrote this department that "it took me five weeks to earn the money to get a picture in the show, and now it's all over and nothing happened." There was the painter who paid for his show but kept finding an "OUT" sign on the door when he went around during scheduled hours to see it. There was the painter who never got his picture back—creating a mystery as to who could have wanted it.

Just as pathetically, there are the many people who pay their money and are happy to have been able to refer to "the time I had my New York show" and to cherish a few frayed lines of review clipped from some strange source. These people, though, are less pathetic and more disturbing as symptomatic of an unhealthy condition in American art that explains the existence of the vanity galleries. The vanity gallery exists because Americans think that anybody can paint, that art has nothing to do with professionalism, and that any exhibition of paintings has, per se, some mystical cultural value deserving of respect.

August 1, 1965

Car-Wash Culture, or,
Big Problems Come in Small Museums

In the summer of 1966 an irreverent article called "Car-Wash Culture" came about as a backfire when a well-placed member of the staff of *The New York Times* asked me to cover an exhibition at the art center in his suburban community. The exhibition was appalling and the activities that were going on at the art center were ghastly. I had to say so, but then in fairness I had to write further about the problems—perhaps insurmountable—that are imposed upon small museums across this country as part of the culture explosion syndrome. The following comments are a fusion of five articles.

Things have come to such a pass in this country that once a community is large enough to support a couple of supermarkets, it begins to think about building an art center. Culture has come to be regarded as a kind of brood hen who, if you build her a lovely nest, will move in and hatch a lot of eggs. Small cities that cannot even support a good restaurant have begun to believe that they can develop a good art museum, and the mothers of healthy children, having become infected with the culture virus, begin to look at their offspring on the baseball lot of a Saturday morning and decide that they should be corralled into painting classes instead.

But the assumption that an art center must add significantly to community life is simply a vapor generated by a mystique relatable to the old biological misconception of prenatal influence. A century ago (and less), pregnant ladies believed that listening to music and regarding works of art and thinking beautiful cultural thoughts would condition the helpless foetus to emerge from the womb under full steam in a direction that would lead it to become a Michelangelo, a Beethoven, or a Byron. In much the same way, an art center is supposed to ooze forth into the communal soil a form of enriching plasma that, perhaps soaked up through the soles of the feet, will do wonders even for the middleaged.

The art centers are much the same whether they serve a town, a suburb, or a neighborhood in a large city, and their proliferation seems to prove that there is so much culture around that it demands multiple vents for release. The opposite is true. The very fact that a thing called an "art center" can exist is the first evidence that art today is increasingly a kind of vermiform appendix in our social system. The art center is an admission that art has been relegated to the position of a pastime for the immature, the aged, the idle or the frustrated. What the art center really is, is an orphan's home.

This would not be so bad, since orphans deserve humane treatment, but the art center is a very bad home for the orphan art. As cultural institutions the art centers do more harm than good. If here and there they rise above the generally debased level of public taste, they more frequently debase the potential level that they are supposed to establish. The argument that art centers may have their faults but that they at least are making a beginning simply cannot be defended. It is not true that a bad job is better than no job at all, when the bad job is presented as a good one, and that is what happens with the art centers.

A typical and flourishing and all-too-well-attended art center not far from Manhattan where ill fortune led this adventurer last week, includes the following divisions within its activities:

A temporary exhibitions gallery, filled at the moment with a one-man show of paintings execrable even by the laxest standards of amateurism, but presented to busloads of school-children, and other innocents, as art, stamped and approved by something called a museum run by people who supposedly should know what they are exhibiting.

A "permanent collection" of about twenty American paintings, of which half a dozen, at the outside, would be exhibitable without acute embarrassment by a museum hold-ing to a standard of quality but desperate for something to put on the walls.

A sales desk where someone, either by extraordinary per-ception or blind fool's luck, has included within a portfolio of reproductions some really excellent ones of old master drawings, the kind of thing that an art center should hunt out for its members as an educational activity. But this port-folio was tucked off in a corner, and the sales counters offered great mountains of objects awful enough to make the sou-venir stands at an airport look like a loan show from the Louvre. The counters were loaded down and the sales cases crammed with an anthology of everything most cheap and corrupt in the way of decorative knickknacks manufactured across the world from Brooklyn to Japan—and into the bar-gain, you could buy practical joke gifts. This was a sales counter that, if it existed somewhere in a community with-out an art center, could be used as an argument for establish-ing one in order to lift the level of taste from rock bottom.

The most popular art classes in this center just now, I am told, are in arc welding, which is having such a boom that the junk yards plug their wares to artists in the local paper. At night the horizons are illuminated with a new flickering aurora borealis as the citizenry gets down to work assembling scrap iron and crumpled bits of automobile bodies, delighted to discover that they are masters of a craft legitimized by aesthetic authority but not at all demanding technically.

The arc welding fad is a neat summary of what is wrong with art center classes. Junk assemblage as a major form of modern sculpture has of course been abused in more respectable quarters, but this abuse neither discredits its use in good hands nor justifies its further abuse at the hands of amateurs. The proper fabrication of junk sculpture demands as highly developed a sense of sculptural form as does stone carving or any other technique less easily imitated by beginners. And in allowing the amateur to play with the technique while ignorant of even elementary aesthetic concepts, the art center makes its typical disgraceful distortion of values, a distortion that makes the centers something worse than merely laughable.

Culture is a matter of education, and the art centers do not educate. They entertain. They give just sufficient directions for using your Fun Kit to create the illusion that you are learning something, but you aren't. You are only blocking by false concepts whatever channels might under proper instruction have been the way to proper understanding. Yet the culture centers cannot be dismissed wholesale. They are part, even if a lamentable part most of the time, of the genuine cultural striving that goes on in small American museums.

Scattered across this country, with concentrations in the Middle West, are dozens upon dozens of small art museums or projects for art museums so new that the ink is hardly dry on their charters. Each one of them needs more money than can be found to run it properly, since every museum in the world needs more money than it can get. Each one of them hopes to accumulate a permanent collection although art objects worth collecting are growing so scarce that major museums are engaged in every kind of power-pull to acquire them at prices that would represent a small museum's total operational budget for several years.

Virtually all of these museums will be run by semi-amateurs with the assistance of total amateurs, and not a one of them will be able to do much good unless the local schools are good in the first place. Their intentions are admirable and the services they can perform are considerable if knowledgeable people can be found, and paid, to direct them, but most of these hopeful institutions are based on a saddening misconception—the idea that if a community can synthesize for itself some of the surface manifestations of culture, then the culture will sink down from the top. Unfortunately, this just does not happen. Even the finest works of art have little value except as decorations or subjects for moony reveries unless they are understood as reflections of the cultures that produced them. And they cannot create this awareness independently.

The trouble with most small art museums is that they see their function as the appreciation and dissemination of something called "beauty," and this can get nobody anywhere. To serve its community the small museum must be an educational institution where the preserved objects, like books in a library, give access to the past in whatever relationship it bears to the present. This is the only defensible reason for spending on an art museum money that could be put into schools—including adult education departments.

But the small art museum even as an adjunct to the educational system can be a pretty shaky affair. The idea that a few second-rate Florentine paintings of the fifteenth century, even if the museum is lucky enough to get them, are going to give a student an understanding of Renaissance humanism is absurd. Like ill-written history books, inferior works of art anesthetize rather than stimulate, because they make the right points in the least interesting fashion. A Renaissance (or other) painting may be indisputably an original, may be in good condition, may even be by a pretty good painter, may be expensive as the very devil, and for all that may be a bore. The whole museum may be a bore, and thus a heartbreak for serious people who have worked hard to create it.

In Blankton, a real city except for this name, the situation is typical except that the interested volunteers are perhaps more energetic and at the same time more thoughtful than most in the creation of an art museum. A manufacturing city with a population, in the 1960 census, of 161,000, Blankton is old enough to have a few mansions from the 1880's, prosperous enough to be tearing them down as fast as possible, and sufficiently unaware of architectural values to destroy without thinking twice some fine examples of indigenous domestic architecture while going out for imported culture.

The art museum, with a small art school attached, is housed at present in a decaying residence of no attraction whatsoever. The lower floor is given over to rental exhibitions from the usual sources in New York, and on the upper floor there are perhaps thirty, perhaps forty, paintings or other objects called the permanent collection.

There is nothing in the collection you would remember for long, although the trash has been cleaned out by a curatorial adviser from Chicago, leaving a residue of some agreeable paintings, including a few by local members of that great band of half-anonymous regional artists who somehow grew all over this country at the turn of the century and left behind so many charming if inconsequential records of our innocence.

Five years ago this seemed to be the sum static total of Blankton's art program. The community has never had anything that could be called a collector or an art patron. But through a combination of the respect for cultural zeal that has been instilled in the citizenry throughout this country and, even more, the hope of bringing back real estate values in the depressed center of the city, a Blankton cultural center now exists—on paper, with plans by a leading architect, and money in the bank.

The heart of the scheme is an auditorium for music and theatricals, but there is also an art museum building in which the present museum would rattle around. The problems of building up and maintaining an effective art museum under the circumstances are so obvious that you can only be appalled upon considering them.

The people who have been working for so long on a hand-to-mouth small-scale operation now find that they have worked themselves into a position where the hand is just as small but the mouth is bigger. Money may be a little easier to get than it was a few years ago but in the new showcase it has to buy relatively more. The committee is also discovering a few of the eternal truths of the museum business, now that it has grown up: that it is easier to get money to build a building than to get money for things to put into it; that it is easier to get money to get things to put into a building than it is to get money to pay a director; that it is easier to get money to pay a director than it is to get money to pay a janitor (and also that it is easier to find directors than janitors); that too many prospective donors want more than their money's worth, such as their names inscribed conspicuously somewhere; that if you accept the obviously phony Rembrandt from old Mrs. Grizzle there is just a chance that she will leave you some money if she ever dies, but an equal chance that she won't.

Blankton has also discovered that at a salary of seven thousand dollars, although it is more in Blankton than it is in New York, your directors will be very young men who are good enough to go somewhere else after a year or two, or not good enough for you to want to keep them. It has discovered that it has no acquisitions program, since one director has wanted to buy modern graphics, another has wanted to buy a single "important" painting with several years' funds, another has wanted to patronize local artists only, whether good or bad, and another has wanted to buy nothing at all and spend everything on temporary shows.

There are talking points for all these attacks, with the exception, I feel, of the one that would concentrate all funds on a very few expensive purchases. Any small art museum's serious program automatically breaks down into three divisions today: it holds temporary exhibitions that are circulated by, primarily, the American Federation of Arts, the Museum of Modern Art and the Smithsonian Institution; it holds home-grown exhibitions of local or regional artists, which are frequently fraught with embarrassments; finally, it tries to acquire a permanent collection, although to do so on a significant scale is virtually impossible.

One small museum that acquired a vigorous director in 1950 boasts that although its collection was "pitiful" (their word) at that time, and although "we do not have money to buy paintings," they have been given a Léger, a Vlaminck, a Vuillard, and a Burne-Jones, and among American artists have paintings by Inness, Sully, Peto, and Henri, as well as a contemporary group that includes a Burchfield. There are also some unidentified seventeenth-century Dutch and Italian and eighteenth-century French paintings.

This sounds good, and the museum is to be congratulated, but let's take a second look. If you live in that city (population, 140,000) and go through the collection once or twice, how many times are you going to be interested in going back? How soon will this collection be exhausted for you? What exploration is there to do? What further revelations are to be found? What new connotations, what interplay, within so small a collection?

Suppose the next sixteen years bring in an equal number of worthwhile pictures, and the next sixteen yet another group, and the next sixteen years a third. Even then, what do you have? (At exactly this point, New Yorkers might ask themselves when they last visited the Frick, with its inexhaustible treasures.)

What you have, out there in Blankton, is a little something, a crust of cultural bread, not even half a loaf. At the cost of perseverance, honest effort, and eternally springing but usually frustrated hope, you have a collection of no real consequence. Your years of effort have gathered together a relative handful of works of art, historically spotty, without theme, aesthetically agreeable perhaps but with no special reason for being, quickly exhaustible even by the most ardent art lovers, too limited in range to be of much educational value to the schoolchildren that a museum likes to serve, and, as symbols of local cultural pride, unlikely to inspire more than a condescending congratulation of the A-for-effort type from visitors.

This merciless judgment is given not in scorn and not in snobbism, but in recognition of the hopeless task of building a significant educational collection of original works of art against the limitation of meager funds. (Any funds not in the many millions are meager for such a project.) Yet the small museum sets out with the pathetic determination to build such a collection. Proud of a dinky minor Léger worth (at the moment) a few thousand dollars, it does not pause to think that whatever the Léger offers as an educational example has already been taught by its adaptation in the best commercial art. The Léger remains a residual pebble on a familiar beach.

Yet the small museum is proud of its Léger because it is an original, and would be horrified at the suggestion that it add to its collection any reproductions of objects it cannot afford. Without a single medieval object in its collection, it would not think of exhibiting a reproduction of the Metropolitan's gerfalcon. This bronze bird, eleven inches high, is either German or Italian, dates from about 1200, was found in Italy in 1925, and was acquired by the Metropolitan in 1947. The museum refuses to set a value on it, but describes it as "one of the finest objects at The Cloisters, and priceless." But a source close to the museum says that if the gerfalcon were to come onto the market today it would bring perhaps a bit less, perhaps a bit more, than a million dollars.

The reproduction costs one hundred dollars, and, since it is cast from the original by direct mold, might almost as well have been cast in 1200 as one of a pair. The collector's thrill of possessing the original can never be approximated by a reproduction, obviously, but for the great throng of the uninitiated, the reproduction (in this case) is not a disfigurement of an unattainable work of art. The late James Rorimer, as director of The Cloisters and then of the museum, was so proud of the mold's accuracy that he used to enjoy putting a cast alongside the original for comparison by visiting museum curators.

It is typical of the misdirection of the small museums that if one of them were given the original bronze, a public holiday would be declared, but that none would think of buying the reproduction and displaying it as the legitimate ambassador of a work of art. This means that as far as the permanent collection is concerned, the small art museum is intent upon being an insignificant approximation of a big museum instead of a working factor in the culture of the community. This approach is self-defeating. After all, even the Metropolitan, at this moment, is not too proud to exhibit some exact reproductions of Byzantine mosaics that are valuable in educational context in ways not represented by originals in the museum's fantastic collections.

Reproductions are extremely dangerous; distorted ones may distort aesthetic and historical values on the grand scale. (Witness the curious ideas the nineteenth century held regarding Greek sculpture, which it knew largely in bad copies and worse restorations and reproductions—ideas that still affect us in spite of everything.) But a director with even an elementary knowledge of his business could work up a collection of reproductions at once inherently beautiful and really valuable as an educational tool, beginning at the Metropolitan, which offers a group of other reproductions in addition to the gerfalcon, and going on to other American and European museums.

Even the museums, however, are not always dependable. The Louvre, for instance, sells with bland indifference some wretched approximations of objects in the collections along with some reproductions as good as the Metropolitan's gerfalcon. And there is a great foul commercial mass of so-called facsimiles and so-called replicas of sculpture that degrade the originals by reduction in size or brutalization of form by copying rather than direct casting from the original. Obviously we are not talking about these when we talk about museum material, and if these comments should send anybody to the gift shop for a small-scale version of Rodin's "Thinker" or Michelangelo's "David," that would be too bad. If some misled individual wants one as a memento, that is another matter.

For less than the price of a single fourth-rate original painting by a popular name, a museum can acquire, in effect, a group of objects it never hoped to own—Amlash and pre-Greek ceramics, African masks, Benin bronzes, Cycladic figurines, pre-Columbian sculpture and goldwork, medieval bronzes and glass, perhaps a Renaissance bronze or two, and a collection of drawings and water colors rivaling some of the great collections in the world when it comes to old masters, and running with few gaps through the history of nineteenth- and twentieth-century art. The trouble is, the director and his board would rather say, "This is our Léger," and point to an incidental effort by a contemporary reputation that drips with blue ribbons, than go against the conventions of museum collecting.

The purchase of a reproduction requires nearly as good an eye as the purchase of an original: in both cases there are those that convince and those that don't. But the convincing reproduction (we insist, against heavy majority opinion) is legitimate museum fare and can be mixed in to make a balanced collection with such originals as the museum is able to acquire.

The reproduction is only an extreme example of the first rule for a small museum trying to build a permanent collection: Never pay as much as five cents for rarity value alone, including the rarity value of a famous name, whether you are buying an Egyptian sculpture or a modern painting. The museum's first job is to collect a representative group of objects that will give some kind of cross section of the history of art, and the rarity of an object can sometimes make it a less effective educational tool than the object that is merely typical.

As an example, a museum would have to pay a stiff price for an Egyptian sculpture inscribed with extraordinary historical references to this or that Pharaoh for whom it was made, whether or not the sculpture simply as sculpture was of extraordinary merit. But the rarity of the inscription or rarity of origin would be of no interest except to Egyptologists, who are hardly numerous in small cities like Blankton.

On the other hand, there are Egyptian sculptures of good quality that can be purchased for one thousand dollars and under, and there are really beautiful fragments of Egyptian bas-reliefs that cost even less than that. Their prices are low for several reasons: Egyptian material exists in quantity; the big museums already have so much that another merely typical example would only take up storage room; private collectors are not interested in owning Egyptian sculpture— partly, perhaps, because they are unaware that it is available or, more likely, as one rich collector remarked when he was offered an exceptionally beautiful Egyptian head for three thousand dollars, "If that's all it costs, it must not be much good." It was very good indeed and was shortly purchased by a not-too-small museum.

The small museum is at a disadvantage because its director seldom knows the New York market—not to mention the international one. It is not entirely a matter of limited funds. If two years ago you had given the director at Blankton the same millions to spend, he would not have had access to the prizes that the Cleveland Museum collected over the same period of time and then put on exhibition in a spectacular celebration of its golden anniversary. Such rarities seldom come onto the open market; they are offered by a very few quiet, powerful dealers to a very few conspicuous, rich museums or collectors.

But outside this super-special market there is the mass of material that, like Egyptian sculpture, one thinks of as rare and expensive, but that can be afforded by anyone who knows where to look and who has an eye for the exceptional piece. These people are rare, and they do not have a chance to develop their potential in Blankton. Blankton, a member of the finance committee says, might collect between a hundred and two hundred thousand dollars for the purchase of art objects in the flush of enthusiasm over their new (and nearly empty) museum building. For that amount of money, a pretty good collection could be started.

But with the cash in his pocket, the typical director would try to hunt out about a dozen prestige items, items of the most obvious, and hence usually most high-priced kind. He might, for instance, buy a de Kooning, and if he did he would be buying a painting by the ranking abstract expressionist. But (although I do not want to cut into Mr. de Kooning's sales) the museum would be making a mistake. A de Kooning sells for many thousands of dollars, but the abstract expressionist movement produced dozens of painters who are equally representative of the theories and virtues of the school and who sell now (or are vainly offered for sale now) for not many hundreds of dollars. Between Egypt and de Kooning, there are parallels all up and down the line.

When you think of the difficulties, it is surprising that new museums continue to appear. That they do, indicates a combination of admirable idealism and extremely tenuous grasp of the problems involved, beyond the money problem, on the part of the hard-working committees in cities like Blankton. Among their sufferings, I think, we must count their poor-relation affiliation with New York.

One New York art dealer of impeccable reputation who can sell you anything from a Rembrandt to a Picasso out of stock on hand, expressed dismay at the suggestion that a small museum might fill in its collection with reproductions, and then, in an incidental reference, revealed that his idea of a "small museum" was the Wadsworth Athenaeum in Hartford, Connecticut, or the Worcester, Massachusetts, Art Museum—two of the most distinguished museums, of any size, in this country, whose directors have been, and still are, among the big names in the field, whose collections are, as the term goes, mouth-watering, and whose ages are respectively 124 and 70.

The only conclusion to be drawn is that in the astral realms in which he operates, shuttling between New York and Europe to do his buying and selling, the dealer cannot conceive of the situation in Blankton, away out yonder somewhere, where a new and really small museum is trying to lift itself up by its bootstraps while keeping its nose above water in a community where there has never been an art collector, where ninety per cent of the population have never seen an original painting by an old master, where eighty-nine per cent don't care whether they ever do see one or not, and where most sensible people still think of art as a stopgap hobby for misfit kids and fading gentlewomen.

Nor does Blankton have problems in common with the "small museum" in a college. As a single primary difference, the staff of the college art museum is integrated with the artists and scholars of the art department and, for that matter, with a full program in the humanities, while Blankton's harassed director, in order to eke out a working group, is likely to have to make do with volunteers whose only qualification for museum work is a willingness to take a crack at it for a little while without pay.

Apparently not very many people who are seriously interested in museums feel that the small (or minnow) museum is worth worrying about one way or another. And as long as it aspires to functions impossible on the scale at which it must operate, perhaps it may be dismissed with indifference. But a representative of one very small museum in the Middle West makes out this case, in a letter:

"I am disappointed that you find so little to admire in the small-museum movement in the United States. I think we are more aware of our limitations than you suspect, although I can speak only in behalf of the one for which I work. We are brand-new. That makes us typical. But during the two and a half years of our existence, we have not striven for what could only be a fourth-rate collection. Instead, we strive to enlarge the experience of our audience, and for most of them we offer the only chance to see works of other times, cultures, and standards. In concrete terms, that means that we must (a) carry on a strong program with the schools and (b) spend our money on loan exhibitions.

The emphasis is on stimulation rather than presenting what-we-can-own as what-should-be-admired. We assume that the appetite for quality, once born, will demand better and better food. If that appetite is to become the common experience of American national life, the small museum has a worthwhile job to do."

With one addition, which we will get to shortly, this would be as good a statement of aims as a small museum could make. It is subject, however, to one great difficulty, in that "works of other times and cultures" are too valuable and too fragile to be shipped around in the rental exhibitions upon which the small museum must depend. As a result, the small museums across the country have become part of one mammoth taste-making circuit radiating from New York, giving disproportionate emphasis to the standard table of aesthetic values formulated by the Museum of Modern Art and proselytized in its rental shows. The quarrel is not with the table the museum has set up but only with its lack of competition. It has been sold so successfully that it is echoed in the great majority of traveling shows available elsewhere and too often echoed at a shoddy level.

This circumstance may be irremediable and may even be majestically inevitable as just one more manifestation of the nature of the modern world, which presses the so-called individual into a standard mold, whether the standard has to do with the kind of detergent he uses or the kind of art he feels free to like. But let's accept the situation for now, assuming that Gresham's law is out of operation and that small museums will grab the best rental exhibitions so enthusiastically that the shoddy ones will go out of circulation.

There remains a major and usually neglected consideration: the small museum's function as a local institution more interested in its own back yard than in the dressing up of its front one. I am quite ready for total opposition on these scores, but I believe that (a) the small museum has an obligation (which should become a pleasure) to hunt out, watch over, and preserve any bits of local popular art, no matter how inconsequential they may seem, that the past, even the very recent past, affords, and (b) that where exhibitions of work by the current crop of local or regional artists are concerned, the museum's motto should be "The hell with New York."

In the first instance:

The museum should be a historical society that gathers a pictorial record of the city (old prints and photographs) from the earliest possible date and keeps it current. Someone should complete a photographic register of local patterns of jigsaw Gothic (as a sample project). When buildings, public or private, are demolished, the director (perhaps with volunteers from the Junior League marching with him in phalanx) should rescue its sculpture and decorative artifacts of all kinds. A snapshot of a family picnic on the Fourth of July, 1910, may wind up as a more valuable acquisition— valuable in several ways—than a portrait of the mayor painted in the same year, although the Historical Committee will also see that this is preserved and documented. And the capitals from the old court house, set up in the museum garden, may wear better (in every way) than more conventional art-sculpture.

As for "The hell with New York," I suggest that every New York or New York-affiliated critic be blackballed as judge of any local or regional art exhibition, and that the blackball be extended to members of such institutions as the Walker Art Center in Minneapolis (this specific reference must be forgiven, and taken as a general one), which so successfully emulate New York standards.

Too many letters, over too many years, have come to this desk from museums that have imported New York (or Chicago, or Minneapolis) judges and have found them condescending, capricious, or merely flummoxed in the face of the local product. And too many lists of prize winners have shown that these judges have judged not on the basis of whatever individual merit the local paintings may have, but on the basis of how closely some local artist is able to imitate the manner of one who is currently fashionable in New York.

Just who is to do the judging? Perhaps laymen, for a change that would not produce more meaningless results. Perhaps professors from nearby colleges who teach something other than art. Perhaps—but as a New Yorker, perhaps I have said enough. After all, you could go on talking forever without affecting the basic problem faced by a museum of any size, which is to find a director and curators with the knowledge, imagination, and energy to make the most of whatever potential their situations offer.

August 14, 21, and 28, September 4 and 11, 1966

6

Reportage

At 12:22 in the afternoon of August 15, 1967, after nearly an hour and a half of music-making, flag-raising, anthem-singing, praying, speechifying, poetry-reciting and telegram-reading in Chicago's Civic Center Plaza, a white ribbon was pulled and, as planned, 12,000 square feet of blue percale fell from the 50 feet and 163 tons of steel called the Chicago Picasso.

The sculpture looked fine, although hardly sensational. It looked even better a couple of hours later when the crowd that had jammed the plaza had cleared away. If there could be any question on other scores, there can be no question as to the success of the sculpture's relationship to its site.

It is not an easy site to satisfy, a plaza 345 feet by 220 feet dominated by the new Civic Center Building, Chicago's highest structure. The sculpture's height and tonnage, however, only partially explain its holding its own within the plaza's scale. It holds its own not as a Gargantua but as an airy, open, even vivacious design. Like a fine bridge (it was, in fact, constructed by the American Bridge Division of the United States Steel Corporation in Gary, Ind.), it combines absolute firmness with an effect of lightness.

The sculpture is no tour de force and its success in place is no accident. But as a creative designer Picasso must share honors with William E. Hartmann, of the architectural concern of Skidmore, Owings & Merrill, who induced Picasso to contribute a maquette for a giant sculpture and who then saw the project through four years that involved repeated consultations with the artist and the raising of three hundred thousand dollars construction expenses from private foundations.

Picasso was supplied with an accurate scale model of the plaza and its buildings and, Mr. Hartmann says, determined the size of the big structure that is, in final analysis, a three-dimensional revamping of a series of drawings done in 1929 and 1930.

Since the acquisition of the sculpture was announced, there has been a great deal of controversy in Chicago, of a nature hardly credible in the year 1967. Picasso's politics and his private life have been thrashed over once more as if they had any connection with the merits or demerits of his sculpture, and those merits and demerits have been evaluated by an aesthetic standard that should have gone up in smoke with the rest of old Chicago in the fire of 1871.

Making allowance for a degree of retardation, the hubbub would have been understandable thirty years ago in a country where the Depression had generated the WPA style

PABLO PICASSO: sculpture in Civic Center, Chicago.
Unveiled in 1967. Fifty feet high. Steel.
Photograph by Declan Haun from Black Star.

—a combination of flat-footed realism, backwoods iconography, and flatulent idealism—as the standard for public monuments, and when the manner that Picasso refurbished for this monument was still new. Even twenty years ago the ruckus would have been understandable, although unexpected in its vehemence, as a residual befogment in a city that had managed, fascinatingly, to reach the top of the heap architecturally while hamstrung in painting and sculpture by some clamorous members of a wealthy rear guard.

But this is 1967, and the fact that so many Chicagoans have been puzzled and angered by this not very advanced sculpture—this sculpture in what has become virtually a classic, if not quite a conservative, twentieth-century style—and that they should be irate for reasons that take us straight back to Sinclair Lewis's *Main Street*—all this leaves one agape. Nothing has been lacking to make the farce perfect except the presence of a native son, William Jennings Bryan, dead these forty-two years but *au courant* half a century ago with the objections raised in Chicago today. He could have summarized in appropriate period oratory the arguments in favor of melting down the Picasso and replacing it with a tribute to, say, pioneer motherhood by any one of the walking dead who compose the National Sculpture Society.

As it was, the Great Commoner found his proxy in an energetic alderman named John J. Hoellen, who appeared at a meeting of the City Council bearing a homemade burlesque of the Picasso and introduced a proposal that the sculpture itself be sent back where it came from and that a statue of Ernie Banks, the Chicago Cubs' baseball star, be erected in its place. Nothing came of this arresting idea except that a motion to censure Alderman Hoellen was introduced and then withdrawn as a bore.

Mr. Hoellen's broad grins in newspaper photographs taken at the time of his fanfaronade, and his ruddy, genial mien during the inauguration exercises, hinted that his and most other objections had been inspired by opportunistic motives (publicity, etc.) or by a simple, misplaced love of horseplay. But a number of letters to this department as well as a continued seething in the Chicago press have indicated that a great many Chicagoans really do loathe their city's new ornament.

The Chicago *Tribune* has editorialized at such length against the sculpture (mind you, it is fine for all the objections to be aired; the only puzzling thing is that such curious objections should be raked up for airing) that on August 17 an advertisement in that paper taken by DePaul University sounded like a paid rebuttal. Morris Barazani, the Vincentian Fathers' artist-in-residence, pointed out that "The fact that Picasso is a Communist and has had a long succession of mistresses has no relation to his art. Art is one thing. Politics and mistresses something else." Also in his "primer for the perplexed" Mr. Barazani said that "Sculpture is not necessarily a representation of a thing; it is a thing all by itself."

This is well said; what is surprising is that it should need saying again. And yet the excitement in Chicago has centered upon the question as to what the sculpture represents.

This opens the back door to the single objection I can see as valid, which is that, rather than not looking enough like something, it looks too much like something. Simply as an object, as "a thing all by itself," the sculpture is a handsome design, an ingenious contrivance at huge scale, a satisfyingly firm piece of engineering that harmonizes in its structure and its material with the new Civic Center building that dominates the plaza. In the openness of its forms it at once occupies a great volume of space—which it has to do in order to hold its own in the large plaza—and yet displaces no space, obstructs no view, in that rarest of treasures, an airy spot in a big city. Because we look not only at but through the sculpture, it takes on an unusual variety of aspects according to our angle of vision. Regarded as a huge abstract stabile (borrowing Calder's term), the Picasso is a brilliant success in situ. The trouble comes when the abstract stabile turns out to be only a semi-abstract sculpture.

The design is abstracted from a woman's head, and as a woman's head it is disturbingly snouted and just plain ugly no matter how interesting it remains as an exercise, a variation on a theme that Picasso has juggled for years. Unfortunately, Picasso's friend, the photographer David Douglas Duncan, has also identified a frontal view of the sculpture, with its snout and its winglike side elements, as a "portrait" of Picasso's long-nosed and long-eared pet Afghan hound, a serious disservice. As a dog's portrait the sculpture would be truly the cheap joke that some Chicagoans feel has been played on them. Or as a piece of symbolism (there has been endless conjecture about this, with Picasso, as always, refusing to comment) the sculpture is reduced to a game of charades.

All of this must be ignored. The Chicago Picasso is an object of a certain size designed in a certain way to ornament a certain place, and as such it is a success. As an expressive work of art beyond its essentially architectural quality, it is understandable only within the context of the arcane convolutions that make modern art an expression of forms of modern thought that not one person in a thousand among those who will see the sculpture every day can understand.

Then, the argument might be, the sculpture should express something that the man in the street does understand. The corollary argument is that the subject should be uplifting. But there is very little evidence that uplifting subject matter in itself has ever uplifted anybody. By the record, public sculpture dedicated to noble ideals can only take on an ironic or at best a sentimentally nostalgic cast after the years during which its ideal is violated by war, corruption, and other un-ideal but persistent social forces—unless, in the first place, it is fine sculpture by the stylistic pattern of its moment. The style eventually becomes the expressive message.

If the Chicago Picasso, once the current foolishness surrounding it wears itself out, becomes an expressive work of art for people in general, it will be because it has captured some of the energy and wild invention that characterize our time, not because it set out to express a social ideal of some kind. If, on the other hand, the years turn it into an eyesore as they have had a way of doing with the majority of public sculptures since 1800, I suspect that the reason will be that the residual bits of representation will have become more and more distracting in a design that even now is marred by them.

August 16 and August 27, 1967

These days, if you are writing on a Monday for a paper that comes out the following Sunday, there is always a chance that you are missing a great story that will turn up during the interval. Who knows, for instance, but that the proper introductory sentence for this article should read, "Everybody's troubles were settled last Wednesday when the world came to an end."

With such wild possibilities in the offing, there is also just the slightest chance that writing on Monday, October 9, for publication on Sunday, October 15, we should be saying, "Well, here we are on the concluding day of the New York Cultural Showcase Festival Fortnight, and it is a pleasure to report that this now-historic event has transformed the city."

But upon the ninth day of an event that we, for one, would like to forget all about, the chances are better that we are safe in beginning, "Well, the Cultural Showcase has come and gone, and the whole thing was a lot of flummery."

This grouchy judgment, even if offered prematurely, has been inherent, from the first, in the nature and in the unfortunately selected name of the project. The lethal flaw behind this effort to make a three-way hybrid out of art, do-goodism, and promotion was its premise that culture is a kind of jam that comes in different flavors—painting, sculpture, music, drama, and tutti-frutti—to be smeared over our daily bread. But what culture really is, is the combination of ingredients in a civilization that determines whether the bread itself is good or bad, full-flavored or tasteless, a nourishing food or a soggy stuffing ingested from day to day for lack of anything better.

To understand the basic absurdity of the Showcase idea, try to imagine Paris or London or Rome adopting it. A relieving note in the embarrassing atmosphere created by this civic effort is that right in the middle of the festivities there were New Yorkers who hadn't even heard (and certainly hadn't felt) that the cultural level had started to soar on October 1 toward a consummation due at the end of two weeks. When you asked their opinion of the Cultural Showcase they would say, "What is it?" and when you told them, they would say, "You're kidding."

Among events listed as "special" in the Showcase's preliminary official announcement there were the following: a black-tie open house at which an obscure female painter acted as hostess at an exhibition of her work; the presentation of some tired movies on art at the Queens Borough Public Library, a worthy enough activity but hardly anything to put in a showcase; an "art talent hunt" and "paint-out" on Central Park Mall, open to anybody, at which an artist-instructor from the Art Students League gave evaluations of work brought to the place or painted on the spot— this being, although not announced as such, a demonstration of the new degradation of art as a picnic for amateurs; a proselytizing outdoor sculpture show, luke-warm in character, thus failing its red-hot advance publicity; and a mish-mash of shows including one on minerals (the cultural connection, apparently considered obvious, was not explained), one on historical transportation devices, and, most puzzling, "Your Stake in the Atom," at the Hall of Science, World's Fair Grounds, Flushing, along with a mass of lectures and concerts and art exhibitions, some of them very good, that had been scheduled long before the Showcase was conceived through some unhappy conjunction of the stars.

The only museum to arrange an exhibition especially for the Showcase was the Whitney, which in its solid, dutiful fashion collected a record of the way artists have painted New York since 1900. It is not at all a bad show. But virtue, once again, was forced to serve as its own reward: at the opening of the exhibition, Thomas P. F. Hoving, of the Metropolitan, happened to mention that back of his museum a grave had been dug by Claes Oldenburg as part of the outdoor sculpture exhibition, and the reporters abandoned the Whitney in a rush for this other attraction. Mr. Oldenburg is well known as a retailer of some of the most highly flavored jam on the market.

It became a matter of the Showcase's pointing with pride to efforts that were antithetical to its sales-pitch concept of art as window dressing and to hell with quality if window dressing can be sold. The Asia House Gallery, with a superb show, stuck a little yellow tag on its information sheet reading "Opening during New York City's Cultural Showcase Fortnight," omitting the words "by coincidence," which would have told the rest of the story. Oddly, Andy Warhol, at our local Temple of the Dionysian Mysteries, the Hudson Theatre, missed a bet for the first time in his life when he failed to attach a Cultural Showcase sticker to his latest blue movie.

O. Henry once called New York Bagdad-on-the-Subway. The Cultural Showcase people would like to change that to the Athens of America. But in their peculiar innocence they have revealed us as Hicksville-on-the-Hudson. In some of its aspects this complicated city is as exotic as the Orient. In others it is indeed the cultural center of America. In yet others, it is a territory inhabited by people who still think of the arts in the terms described in *Main Street* so long ago. Those were essentially the terms of the Showcase. Oh, Sinclair Lewis! Oh, Carol Kennicott! Oh, Gopher Prairie! Oh, New York—Gopher Prairie Irredenta!

October 15, 1967

Ginevra de' Benci, the Ill-Natured Debutante

Washington, March 16—Looking terribly out of sorts and more than a little out of drawing—the two sides of her face have never matched—Leonardo da Vinci's "Ginevra de' Benci" received the press this afternoon at the National Gallery of Art preliminary to beginning permanent residence in public when the museum opens at 10 A.M. tomorrow morning. As a debut, the news conference could hardly be expected to hold surprises and yielded none during the fifteen minutes that it lasted.

The painting has been installed in the center of a small gallery of its own, described as a "lobby," between a garden court and a sculpture hall, where it can be seen front and back. The screen constructed to hold it is stretched with red velvet, and the two surfaces of the painting are protected by Plexiglass structures described as "bullet resistant." Standing alongside, John Walker, director of the gallery, outlined the five reasons "why this is one of the most precious paintings in the world."

LEONARDO DA VINCI: *Ginevra de' Benci,* ca. 1480.
15⅛″ x 14½″. Oil, resin, and tempera on wood.
Courtesy of the National Gallery of Art, Washington, D.C.;
Ailsa Mellon Bruce Fund.

First, he said, because Leonardo ranks among "the great-est of human geniuses" and second, because he painted very few pictures. Name and rarity, sufficient explanation for monetary preciousness, were thus established, but Mr. Walker does not like to think of the picture in monetary terms and has been begging, in vain, for just one news story that does not mention the rumored price of five million—or six.

Third, he said, the painting "is one of the examples that show Leonardo's unequaled ability to model three-dimensional form," and he called attention to "the fantastic subtlety and delicacy of the transitions from light to shade in the cheek." A stickler could have objected, however, that in his early work Leonardo had not yet developed the form of softened modeling called "sfumato," which was his important contribution to the technique of describing form.

Fourth, Mr. Walker pointed out, "this painting on wood panel is remarkably preserved." Forgetting that it has been chopped off at the bottom, this is true. What is left is in much better condition than the Mona Lisa.

Fifth, Mr. Walker referred to the "miracle of psychological insight" by which Leonardo expressed "the somber side of personality," and pointed out that "the experience of my colleagues and myself has been that this picture has a mysterious way of growing on you the more often you see it." This seems to be true. At least the picture looked better to this observer today than it looked the only other time he saw it, which was about the year 1937, upon which occasion he took a dislike to it. It also looked better and better minute by minute during the press session, especially dur-

ing a preliminary period of milling around when it was not
overlighted for the cameras.

But whether or not it is a really great painting is a real
question. Without Leonardo's name to inspire initial respect followed by the kind of concentrated attention that
would give increasing fascination to any good portrait, it
would probably only be one of dozens of Renaissance portraits—including at least a dozen already in the National
Gallery—that individuals might regard as a favorite or
antipathetically, or might respond to in no way at all.
All response, however, is preconditioned for the public.
"Ginevra de' Benci" is rapidly becoming, like the Mona
Lisa, a legend rather than a painting, and hence any independent response to its inherent virtues and shortcomings is
obscured.

The press had very little to ask about the painting, and
the first question naturally was as to the price paid Prince
Franz Josef II of Liechtenstein. Mr. Walker said he wouldn't
answer that one. The second question was, Why wouldn't
he? His answer was that he didn't want people to think of
the painting in terms of cost.

Perhaps, eventually, the cost may be forgotten. Less
likely, the picture might be judged, sometime, just as itself.
"The thing that bothers me," one critic grumbled to another
on the way out, "is the way all the school kids are going to
be herded in front of this little picture and told to get all
inspired."

The picture is not inspiring. It is a beautiful object in
pattern and color, a curious representation of a rather unpleasant personality, and by historical identification an extremely important work of art. That is a high score, so there

really is no good reason not to give "Ginevra de' Benci" a patient welcome while we wait for the exaggerated excitement to die down.

The painting is scheduled for eventual placement where it belongs—in a gallery along with others, not enshrined.

March 17, 1967

Florence After the Flood

FLORENCE, Italy—Nearly a month after the flood, the Florentine disaster may have faded in the consciousness of even those people who love the city best, but here the disaster is still current. The city remains in a state of siege. The besieger is mud.

The extent of the losses has been (and to a large extent still is) conjectural, based on early reports from Italians and from very lively and very vocal visiting Americans who obviously could not be specific but who could not help being emotional, sometimes in the direction of hope, but usually in horror. Even now, the immensity of the ruin is beyond anything expected.

We usually forget that Florence, in addition to being the small medieval and Renaissance city lying on the lowest banks of the Arno, is a big modern industrial city stretching for miles around, many feet above this unparalleled concentration of museums and historical monuments. As you come into Florence, you go through the miles of this anonymous modern city, and everything looks fine. It is not until you get into the disaster area, armed with a pass that you hope will get you into the morasses that used to be your favorite spots, that the shock begins.

As a concession to friends who swore you would need them, after all these weeks, you have brought along rubber boots. It is apparent even at the starting point, the Piazza del Duomo, where things are relatively cleared up, that you need them, and before long they are coated with ooze and slime up to their tops. As you walk through this mess, you keep checking the flood level by the ugly deposit of fuel oil on the walls alongside. And before you have gone very far, it has risen as high as 12 feet above your head.

And there is always the mud. It is exactly the color of the rest of Florence—a tawny ochre, but this aesthetic unity doesn't help much. The most pathetic sight here is also one of the most frequent: out of the dank interior of a ruined shop, where the oil line is well above the door, a figure will emerge carrying a bucket of mud. He is the shopkeeper, who during the first days could not even begin to clear away the feet-deep deposit because there was simply no place to put it. Now his street is sufficiently cleared for him to make a pile of mud and the debris of such of his shop fittings as were not carried away, which will eventually be cleared by the army, in almost as piecemeal a fashion as the shop-keeper deposited it. In the narrowest streets, the mechanical scoops operated by the army are necessarily of miniature size.

The man with the bucket of mud is the most pathetic sight here, but the most tragic sight is an expected one, Cimabue's great "Crucifix," with seventy to eighty per cent of its surface either washed away or irretrievably ruined. It lies like a corpse on a catafalque on an improvised scaffold-ing in the museum of the Church of Santa Croce, where it hung while the place filled with eighteen feet of water. You have known that the Cimabue was ruined, but when you see it lying there, sodden, stained, and peeling, you realize fully that this is the end of a great painting that has been revered as a work of art and as a religious object for seven hundred years.

And yet its tragedy is not the most appalling of all. This comes at the National Library, the most important single repository of Italian manuscripts going back to the twelfth century, books, records, and incunabula, including collections that have been only partially tapped as historical source material. You see the rooms where students are working at the job of drying the books, interleaving them with blotting paper, page by page, and you know that this process is being duplicated in other Italian cities where salvageable books have been sent.

But it may take hours to interleave a single volume of the tens of thousands that are waiting. And there are many tens of thousands that are not exactly waiting. The halls of the library are filled with soggy mountains of books sprinkled with sawdust to absorb some of the moisture but sprouting and smelling of mold.

With a flashlight it is possible to go down into the lower vaults of the library. The bent and collapsing racks rise above as much as a foot of thick, brown soup, the remainder of a deposit that filled them to the ceiling. Sloshing through in your boots, you are aware of an unfamiliar texture underfoot, gummy and spongy, too firm to be mud, not firm enough to be the floor. You are walking over a layer of books, a paste made of mud, paper, cloth, vellum, and leather.

If all estimates of losses here, including official ones, have been half guesswork at this stage, the loss at the National Library will never be more than guessable. Sections of the library's catalogue are part of the mush, and carry with them such record as there was of books that could include manuscripts awaiting discovery, which have now reverted to the condition of primeval ooze.

These days in Florence, when you look at the Arno, which is still boiling although contained within its banks, it is difficult to feel the old affection for it as a stream—we have seen it in summer reduced to a trickle—that watered the roots of modern Western culture. The disaster of the National Library is repeated wherever historical material was stored in the flood area. Not content with flooding the basement vaults where records were stored and the lower floors where they were displayed, the river collected an extra dividend by collapsing the floors of the rooms in the Strozzi Palace where the Vieusseux library of Romantic literature was housed. Dumped into the ravenous water, the library of 250,000 volumes is apparently a total loss. Similarly, the fragile treasures of the Archaeological Museum are now, by report, part of a dank jumble of broken cases and ruined construction.

The State Archives, with a staggering fifty-million-document collection from the thirteenth to the nineteenth century, have been thirty per cent saved; no one knows about the rest. In church after church, everything from illuminated manuscripts to the parish records seems to have been kept in the most vulnerable spots. The libraries of all departments of the University of Florence have suffered.

Even if half of the lost material (a wildly generous figure) is available elsewhere or in photographs (very little was microfilmed), the loss represents the disappearance of a mine for the exploration and re-evaluation of Western culture that had seemed inexhaustible. For the Florentines this loss is at least as disastrous as the more dramatically publicized losses of painting and sculpture. It is a loss in an area where intellectual, spiritual, and practical values overlap.

Florence can live well enough on its income from industries (it is a center of furniture manufacture and leather processing, among others) and from its vastly profitable tourist trade after the town is cleaned up. But the Florentines have always been proudest of their position as the focal point of Italian thought and history. Even Rome has been more nourished by Florence than nourishing to it. And while Florence has always been fond of tourists, it has taken most pride in the scholars who come here for research. There is great unease, now, on this score. It is not likely that Florence will become exactly a cultural ghost town (tourists have nothing to do with culture), but it will be many months before Florence knows even approximately where the flood has left it as a source of intellectual supply, and it will take years to accept as routine whatever changes the disaster has imposed on the city's intellectual life.

By a kind of perverse luck, the bad weather that continued to plague Florence after the flood has been something of a godsend in the emergency treatment of damaged paintings. The sun appeared only fitfully; the air was chilly and damp with little change from day to day, which comes close to being a definition of conditions that the conservators would have demanded, if they could have, for the hospitalization of paintings rescued from total drowning.

Pending their removal to other quarters, the paintings have been laid out on improvised supports in the dampest portions (usually rooms that had been flooded, in plentiful supply) of churches, chapels, museums or public buildings, where the soaked walls and slimy floors assure a humidity close to saturation. This humidity is necessary for the panel paintings of the fifteenth century and earlier that represent the most fragile members of the casualty list.

Until the use of oil on canvas became general in Italy, paintings were executed on thick wooden panels covered with a thin coat of gesso, a type of fine-grained plaster bound with gelatine. Under normal conditions such paintings deteriorate very little. Their great enemy is drastic change in humidity or temperature, which causes the wooden base and the gesso surface to expand or contract at different rates, so that the gesso, carrying the painting with it, chips, peels, and flakes away under the stresses created.

The problem here since November 4 has been to prevent the soaked panel paintings from drying out until the process could be properly controlled. There have been two hazards —warm, dry weather, or a sudden drop well below the freezing point where the thermometer has hovered. Every time the sun has broken out, Florentines in general have cheered, but conservators have trembled. A sudden hard freeze would be even worse, and although this would be unlikely at this time of year, it is not impossible. Conservators believe that the improbable conjunction of natural violences that produced the flood could have established a precedent for further abnormal behavior of the elements.

Within a week, the panel paintings are expected to be

safely under treatment in the Limonaia, a cross between a palace and a greenhouse in the Boboli Gardens. The Limonaia is ordinarily the winter home of the lemon and orange trees and the cactuses that are moved into the gardens for the summer. This winter, ornamental botany will be sacrificed to fine art.

The Limonaia provides a large work space adaptable to humidity and temperature control, and work on the installation of heavy equipment and some interior remodeling is running neck and neck with the concurrent promise of fine weather and threat of a freeze. In their new quarters, the panel paintings will be dried out systematically and slowly over the coming months, beginning with a humidity close to one hundred per cent.

Fresco paintings have had good and bad luck. In the museum—formerly the refectory—of Santa Croce, Taddeo Gaddi's "Last Supper," which was entirely covered by the same eighteen feet of water that drowned the Cimabue, has been cleaned and seems none the worse for the entire experience, but there will be ineradicable oil stains on other, more porous frescoes.*

The oil, which rode on top of the flood from the burst tanks of Florentine heating systems, was a major culprit everywhere. Soaking into soft stone, it has made discolorations too deep to be removed. The marble sculptures by Baccio Bandinelli ornamenting the altar enclosure of the Duomo are among the highly polished marbles that were covered by oil film but now look fresher than ever after a

---

* Gaddi's "Last Supper" did not remain long in apparently happy condition. As it dried out, a salty deposit obscured its surface, and extensive treatment was required.

bath of soap and water. There are many and contradictory problems. The water that darkened some stones bleached others. To a non-technical eye, it seems to have been a flood that respected no rules of consistency.

The most publicized damaged sculptures have been Ghiberti's bronze "Doors of Paradise" on the Baptistry. They stand in place now with five of the ten panels missing, two of them from the top, well above water level. Contrary to the general impression, the panels were not ripped loose by the force of the water. They were dislodged by the impact of the doors against the jamb when the doors were violently burst inward.

While the waters rose in the Piazza del Duomo, Monsignor Alberto Poli stayed in his building on a balcony, like a captain on the bridge of his sinking ship. The water spurted through the cracks of the doors in jets like those from a fire hose, until at last the doors were forced inward by the pressure, as were the earlier doors by Andrea Pisano. (The third set of doors, also by Ghiberti, look today as if they had never even seen water.) The impact of the huge bronze frames against the stone jambs, and probably some subsequent banging back and forth, dislodged the five Ghiberti panels and split one of the Pisano doors (the one to the right) down its middle lengthwise, but with no serious damage to the relief sculptures that run in pairs along this line.

All five Ghiberti panels and the Pisano panel, with a few fragments, were retrieved and are now in an office of the Museo del Opera del Duomo. They are an unholy mess of gummy oil that will have to be cleaned off before some inevitable dentings and scratchings and possibly some small losses become apparent, but the damage does not seem serious.

For people who love Florence, the good or ill fortunes of favorite monuments are cause for relief or sorrow, but one aspect of the situation escapes general attention. The chemical action of salts in the mud and the ugly discoloration of the oil will have full time to take permanent effect on the innumerable little bits of unimportant carving and stone work that, spotted here and there, have been a constant delight.

Florentines are busy trying to get their city back into exactly its pre-flood condition—they are not interested in repairing damages in any other way. But the damage to the small, anonymous stones of Florence will change the aspect of the city for anyone who has loved it as an entity where every fragment is identified in brotherhood with the masterpieces.

Published December 5, 1966. Written somewhat earlier.

Epilogue

It comes as a pleasant surprise to the author that this book on art and its public in the mid-1960's can end on an unforced note of cheer. A few weeks after the appearance of "Looking Forward to Not Getting All Wrought Up This Season, Thank You," the article that serves as an introduction to this volume and was in itself rather hopeful, circumstances justified the following happy comments, which appeared on November 3, 1968, under the title "Inside and Outside Gresham's Law." It serves as our envoi.

Checking against the Columbia Encyclopedia to be sure I had it right, I discover Gresham's Law stated thus: "When depreciated, mutilated, or debased coinage (or currency) is in concurrent circulation with money of high value in terms of precious metals, the good money automatically disappears."

The art circus of the 1960's has indicated that Gresham's Law could be paraphrased to apply to art, thus: "When shoddy, sensational, or merely second-rate art is exhibited and publicized concurrently with art of high merit in terms of proved aesthetic and historical values, the good exhibitions automatically disappear."

By the end of last season this seemed to have happened finally in New York. The record for several years past had shown an increasing majority of the best exhibitions origi-

nating outside New York, with New York museums reject-
ing invitations to participate in them. It had come to the
point where you had to go to Boston, Philadelphia, Buffalo,
Cleveland, Detroit, and the West Coast to check up on the
difference between a museum and a discothèque. The low
point came last February when the Metropolitan exhibited
James Rosenquist's "F-111" in an error of judgment that,
looking back, seems also to have been the turning point.
(In retrospect, too, we can see that our greatest museum's
error at least supported the theory of art as prophecy, since
the scandal of the Metropolitan's lapse anticipated the scandal created by the performance of a miserable aircraft.)

The rebound from this nadir has been sudden, and most
spectacular at the Metropolitan itself. There and elsewhere
in the city a galaxy of superb exhibitions has burst upon us,
exhibitions of such quality that Gresham's Law has been
thrown into reverse. Everybody has been so busy getting
around to see good things that nobody has had time for the
junk. Presumably it is still with us, but the only trashy show
to have attracted any attention has been Robert Rauschenberg's at the Museum of Modern Art. Mr. Rauschenberg, a
bright but capricious talent, has cooperated by producing
an unqualified fizzle to help turn Gresham's Law inside out.

Sunday before last, October 20, the attendance record
for a single afternoon was broken at Asia House when
more than 1,100 people came to see the current exhibition
of ancient Chinese bronze ritual vessels—rather specialized
fare. On October 24, with nearly four weeks to run, the
closing date having been extended to November 19, the
Metropolitan's show of Italian frescoes had brought in
145,283 visitors,* about twenty-five per cent of the museum's

* At the closing of the show, 377,171 people had viewed the frescoes.

total attendance, paying to see the frescoes except on one free day a week. The catalogue, which is a scholarly reference work, has gone into its third printing with about ten per cent of the visitors buying it.

Figures like these have nothing to do with the kind of museum attendance figure that includes the blank-eyed wanderer with an afternoon to kill. These people know what they want to see—the pure gold of art coinage. As long as it is around they have no use for what is "depreciated, mutilated, or debased." They have discovered, or have known all the time, that to see great art of any period with a fresh eye is worth infinitely more than to follow the rat race of current novelties with a—necessarily—jaded one.

This does not mean that great exhibitions exclude contemporary art, although New York's at the moment include none.* The Albright-Knox Gallery's "Plus by Minus" survey last season was proof enough that the gold is there for exhibition. But it does mean that our wearisome exploitation of the new for the sake of the new has debased our standards for contemporary art simply because there is not enough of high quality to fill the inflated exhibition programs that the museums have saddled themselves with. Which may be why the Guggenheim, a museum of modern art, has devoted the entire first half of this season to ancient Peru.

Last week the Metropolitan came through with another superb exhibition, "Medieval Art from Private Collections," at the museum's medieval branch in Fort Tryon Park, The Cloisters. The assembled objects—sculpture, stained glass, paintings, drawings, and enamels—are a revelation of the

---

* —but three weeks later the Museum of Modern Art opened its excellent "The Machine As Seen at the End of the Mechanical Age."

quiet, golden collecting that goes on beneath the razz-ma-tazz of fashion selling and publicity buying. The selection was made by Carmen Gomez-Moreno, Associate Curator of Medieval Art and The Cloisters, who also prepared the perfect catalogue. (How pleasant to know that to describe a catalogue as a sound, scholarly work this season is to give it a send-off rather than the kiss of death.) Response to the exhibition has been so great that the Metropolitan is running special buses from its Fifth Avenue door to The Cloisters.

With collectors like these, with curators like these, with museum sponsorship like this, and with a responsive public such as we have been having, why worry about that flurry of counterfeit bills blowing around in the gutter?